From Pew to Pulpit

From Pew to Pulpit

A Beginner's Guide to Preaching

CLIFTON F. GUTHRIE

Abingdon Press
Nashville

FROM PEW TO PULPIT
A BEGINNER'S GUIDE TO PREACHING

This book is printed on acid-free paper.

Library of Congress Cataloging-in-Publication Data

Guthrie, Clifton F. (Clifton Floyd)
  From pew to pulpit : a beginner's guide to preaching / Clifton F. Guthrie.
    p. cm.
  Includes bibliographical references.
  ISBN 0-687-06660-3 (pbk.: alk. paper)
1. Preaching.   I. Title.

BV4211.3.G88   2005
251—dc22

                                                         2005016450

05 06 07 08 09 10 11 12 13 14—10 9 8 7 6 5 4 3 2 1

MANUFACTURED IN THE UNITED STATES OF AMERICA

To the students

of Bangor Theological Seminary

whose journeys from pew to pulpit

have been an inspiration

Contents

Acknowledgments

I want nothing more out of this book than for it to be of use to those who are making a first journey from pew to pulpit. I am grateful to all the students in my preaching courses and workshops who previewed and commented on several of the chapters and willingly lent me their preaching stories to use as anecdotes. They bravely tolerate strange teaching experiments (some of which involved dancing and preaching through brick walls) to help us discover together ways that let even reserved and frozen Mainers become passionate proclaimers of the gospel.

I also want to acknowledge the members of Belmont United Methodist Church in Lithonia, Georgia, with whom I had the privilege of preaching for two years back in the 1980s. Like many smaller congregations, that church has since had to close its doors due to a religious economy that favors slickness and size over the kind of genuine Christian community I encountered there. While contemplating their doubtful future as a congregation, the patriarch of the church once admitted, "I suppose our main ministry is helping new preachers learn how to preach." Their willingness to perform this ministry with me, I have no doubt, is the reason I am teaching preaching today. So to all the smaller churches in Georgia, Maine, and in between who hear student preachers so eagerly and carefully, I wish to express my heartfelt thanks. In your midst, God gives birth to the Word.

Introduction

To keep this book inexpensive, up to date, and flexible, I have developed a corresponding Web site: www.pewtopulpit.com. Here you will find recommended resources for the new preacher, the most useful Internet sites for Bible study, information about how to select a good study Bible, and other suggestions that could not be included in the book. At many points along the way, I will refer you to related links on this Web site for further information.

This book is meant for folks who are new to preaching, people whose backsides have not forgotten the feel of the pew. There are many excellent preaching textbooks out there that can guide you in the intricacies of biblical exegesis, sermon development, and delivery techniques. But unlike the vast majority of them, this book does not assume that the person seeking help with preaching is someone who:

1. Has the luxury of time and money to pursue a seminary education
2. Has or will someday have at his or her disposal a solid and up-to-date library of Bible and other preaching resources;
3. Is ordained or is training to be ordained
4. Must preach every single week to the same congregation
5. Personally identifies with the professional role of the clergy

You may indeed be all of these things, but this book does not assume that you are. The call to preach comes in too many different ways and to too great a variety of people these days to make easy assumptions about the people who respond to it. There are lay speakers, local deacons, youth workers, parish nurses, Sunday school superintendents, student pastors, local pastors, interns—any and all of whom may be called to preach. There is a large church nearby, for example, whose new pastor has decided that when he is absent it makes more sense to ask members of the congregation to preach than to invite clergy who would be unfamiliar to the congregation. There is a cluster of four churches in rural Maine who collectively are able to cobble together enough money to pay a pastor. But because the pastor can only lead three services on a Sunday, each church conducts one service a month itself and calls on lay members to preach.

Other churches that do employ full-time clergy are finding that more and more laity participate in in-depth Bible study programs such as the United Methodist DISCIPLE courses, or the Episcopal *Education for Ministry* (EFM), and that some of them emerge from these studies with a burning passion for ministry that begs to be shared with a congregation gathered for praise. With such a feast of insight available to the congregation, suddenly the idea of reserving the pulpit for one voice Sunday after Sunday seems less appealing. Clergy and churches are discovering that when they call upon lay preachers, the full-time clergy preach better themselves and their sermons seem fresher.

Sometimes the call to preach knocks people to the ground and turns their lives around, as it did Paul on the road to Damascus. At other times the call is as ordinary as the call to fix the plumbing in the fellowship hall. It is just something important that needs to be done, and someone needs to step forward if we are to continue being the church. "Well, Bob," says one church member to another at the board meeting, "you're a good Sunday school teacher, why don't you preach next Sunday?" Here God's voice does not boom at you from the clouds, but speaks through the ordinary grace of people who know you and sense that you have a testimony to give.

Whatever form your call to preach takes, formal or informal, out of institutional need or a Voice pressing on your insides that you can no longer ignore, welcome to your new life as a preacher.

In-Between People

Chances are that if you are reading this book you feel that you are somewhere in between the pew and the pulpit. Preaching is strange new territory for you, or perhaps you have never preached at all. Some of you reading may be preaching regularly but haven't had the time to think deeply about how you are doing it. Sunday to Sunday you feel as if you are flying by the seat of your pants and the grace of God. This method worked well for a few weeks, but now the desperateness of it has taken its toll.

Being an in-between person is a good thing. The people of Israel were exiles and wanderers; Jesus had nowhere to lay his head. In-between people have the most interesting stories to tell and the deepest need to rely on grace. Some would even say that it is only in the in-between times that we are free enough from the structures and strictures of ordinary life to hear God's voice.

New preachers know this in their bones. You have your feet on the ground and fresh memories of hearing sermons that zing in the ears and move the body to praise. You also know what it is like to sense the energy draining from a room during a bad sermon: averted eyes, shuffling papers, and slumped backs. Plus, if you're a new preacher, you haven't yet fallen into ruts or become comfortable in the role. Folks in the pews still see an in-betweener as one of their own. They still tell off-color jokes in your presence and don't yet always ask you to say grace.

I'm an in-betweener too. After finishing seminary, I preached for six years as a United Methodist pastor in the South. In 1993 I became an Episcopal layperson and pursued a more academic life. In the years since then I have heard far more sermons than I have preached. I am still invited to preach regularly, but unless I happen to be a guest preacher or visiting another congregation, most Sundays you will find me sitting with my family in the fourth pew on the left in a small-town church in Maine.

I've learned as much or more about good preaching in these past dozen years than I did when I was preaching every week. For one thing, I get to hear all kinds of preachers instead of just one: myself. I sense the reaction of a congregation more immediately than I did before. I notice the small things that you just can't see very well from the pulpit: the hesitant slide of the wife's hand across the pew cushion toward her husband when the sermon touches on marriage problems, the small sighs of the veteran behind me when the pastor preaches another sermon on war, and the furtive glances passing among the folks in the back who sometimes seem not to be listening at all.

Firsthand News

If you have sat in the pews for a long while listening to sermons, you know what a gift it is to hear a thread of your own story lifted up as sacred speech. You also know how demeaning it is to have your complex experiences of God, family, community, and world reduced to a formula or ignored completely. The gospel that we are called to preach is good news to real people, people just like us in their griefs, memories, and loves. This is perhaps the biggest spiritual challenge in moving from pew to pulpit: to remember what it is like to be a hearer of sermons. Will your preaching honor our complex stories, the many differences we have, and the things we hold in common? Will it raise the deepest chords of our common life to God?

Emerging writers are told to start by writing what they know. Emerging preachers can benefit from the same insight. Preach what you know about the density of your own relationship with God and neighbor and your sermons will be life giving. Give us your testimony and help us believe.

Jesus met a man who was beset by a legion of demons. After Jesus cast them into the pigs, the healed man wanted to follow Jesus, but Jesus told him instead to "Go home to your friends, and

EXERCISE: WHAT IS YOUR "FIRST-HAND NEWS"?

To preach well it is important for you to know the contours of your own faith journey. Take some time now to write a spiritual autobiography. Some people find it helpful to draw a map or a graph, indicating high and low points along the way.

These questions may also help:

- In what tradition(s) or religious culture(s) were you raised?

- Have you changed your denomination or religion over the years?

- What were the key turning points in your life of faith?

- Did you have one powerful conversion experience, or did you grow in faith gradually?

- When did you start reading the Bible seriously?

- When were you baptized? What does that mean for you today?

- What particular worship services or sermons stand out in your memory? Why?

- When did your religious beliefs or practices change significantly? Why?

- Have you had any important spiritual mentors? What did you learn from them?

- How do you practice your faith today? Be specific—and honest!

- What is God doing in your life these days?

tell them how much the Lord has done for you, and what mercy he has shown you" (Mark 5:19). Jesus met a woman at a well and asked her a simple question about her life. Afterwards, she ran into town, wondering aloud whether she had met the Messiah. In the end, the story goes, "many Samaritans from that city believed in him because of the woman's testimony" (John 4:39).

Both the man and the woman in this story discovered the key to good preaching: it is telling people what you know. Sister Lawson, as the new local pastor of an African Methodist Episcopal Zion church in Buffalo had it right when she said that the essence of her preaching ministry is: "Just telling people how good God has been to me, and letting them know that he is there for them, too."

The Spirit's Gift

"Pursue love, and strive for the spiritual gifts, and especially that you may prophesy." (1 Corinthians 14:1)

Some people believe that you can't really learn to preach at all; it's simply a matter of being gifted by the Spirit or not. I believe that the Spirit offers us gifts, but I don't believe that normally God works by zapping unsuspecting people with talent from on high. Paul's own words cited above to the Christians in Corinth struggle toward a paradox: on the one hand, the gifts are given by God alone; on the other, we are told to strive for them, especially prophecy. How do you strive for something that is a gift?

This paradox rings true. Anyone who has attended church for a while knows that the Spirit's gifts to a church are complicated. It can be like going to a high-school musical: there are plenty of kids on stage who have been told by their parents and teachers that they are more gifted than they really are. Yet we go crazy over their enthusiastic rendition of "There's a Place for Us" because those are our children up there and our love for them gives us more generous ears than a Broadway talent scout. We especially applaud those kids who perhaps don't sing or act so well but throw themselves into the role beaming with energy. At the local level, it is often the intention that makes the difference, not the talent.

Preaching can be the same. The Spirit may call on certain people in our congregations to be preachers but they may not be very good at it. But talent is not really the issue. In 1 Corinthians 12, Paul doesn't suggest that the Holy Spirit gives us talents, but gifts. These are never for ourselves, but for the sake of the whole Christian community. The right intention for preachers to have is love, as Paul says flat out in the thirteenth chapter. It will be remarkable even to folks who are outside the church just how far this intention will go in preaching. Mediocre preachers whose meager gifts are used for the sake of building up the community in love will make a profound difference in people's lives. Naturally talented speakers whose sermons reflect only their own needs already have their reward. It is a simple point to make at the beginning of a discussion about preaching, but it must never be forgotten: Preaching is an act of Christian lovemaking with words.

Yet to judge from their weighty tomes, many preaching teachers apparently believe that teaching preaching is an enormously complicated matter. You must exegete the Bible like a professor, have the contemporary insight of a network news analyst, write stories like a Pulitzer prize winner, have the wit and confidence of a stand-up comedian, and a voice like James Earl Jones. Learning to preach can easily become a desperate attempt to ramp up all these skills—with the hope of preaching well fading away the more one reads about it and the more that hope is replaced by anxiety.

At times my own teaching of preaching has unfortunately communicated this attitude. I once heard a student say at the end of a semester that he thought he was a pretty good preacher before, but that now he had taken the class it seemed much harder than he had thought. He confessed that he had lost confidence rather than gained it by learning about a sermon's focus, function, and form. He could preach OK when he was just being himself, he went on, but as soon as he tried to do what the experts told him (including me, I suppose), it seemed false and unnatural.

Like other students, however, he eventually came out of this false struggle between spontaneity and study. He recovered his sense of God's gift and calling and his hearers reported that his sermons were clearer and more powerful for the hard work he had put in.

Every gift is like this to some degree. The artist may feel that her spontaneity suffers from the rigors of art school attention to brush strokes, style, and form. But eventually she comes out on the other side integrating the advice of seasoned practitioners while retaining the originality of her unique inspiration.

> Judy, a new preacher, reported:
> "Being an X–ray tech, my training centers around tasks to operate a machine. I think I have been in the same mind-set about writing sermons. I think I thought there must be a 'right' and 'wrong' way to do them. I have learned that there are as many varied styles as there are people and situations. Life, and God's action in the world, is too fluid to think there could be some static program for a sermon."

This book takes you through one process of developing a sermon that I have found reliable over the years. It is similar to what I use in my classes. To judge by the fine quality of the sermons they preach to one another, it is one that my students seem to find helpful. But practice is the best classroom, and the best preaching students are the ones who learn from their experiences what works best for them. So take what works for you and leave the rest. Most important, trust the intuition that drove you to pick up this book and spend time reflecting on your preaching ministry. And trust the Spirit that brought you to this ministry in the first place.

Curious Callings

espite our tendency sometimes to think otherwise, there
never was a day when all of God's preachers were impos-
ing men with booming voices and unwavering confidence in their calling to ministry. Rather, both scripture and
church history show us that preachers' bodies, natural abilities,
and inner convictions vary widely. They come to the task with
strength and frailty, certainty and doubt, talent and inadequacy.
In other words, they are people like us. Yet the stereotypes continue to limit the power of the gospel in our churches and in ourselves. You new preachers who are blessed (or cursed) with
unshaken confidence that God has called you to pulpit ministry
need not read this chapter. The rest of us may benefit from a little review of the many and curious ways that God has called very
ordinary people like you and me to preach.

Reluctant Prophets

The Bible is full of reluctant preachers. In fact, God would
seem to specialize so much in speaking through hesitant people
that it's almost wise to be downright suspicious of preachers-to-be

who are champing at the bit. Moses worried himself sick at the burning bush: "But suppose they do not believe me or listen to me, but say, 'The LORD did not appear to you' " (Exodus 4:1). Samuel was a small boy who heard voices in the night and was afraid to tell the old priest Eli about his dreams (1 Samuel 3:2-18). Isaiah's vision of God's holiness was so overwhelming that he wouldn't speak until his own sinful lips were made clean (Isaiah 6:1-8). Jonah was so reluctant a preacher that he hopped on a boat, tried to get others to drown him, and was swallowed by a fish. Even when his five-word sermon (in the Hebrew text) caused the whole city of Nineveh to repent, he went out and sulked (Jonah 4).

In the throes of sermon preparation you may be hit by a freight train of self-doubt: who am I to stand up and preach? However I got to this place, it must be a mistake. The people who invited me are going to wonder what in the world they were thinking!

"Deep in my heart I still believe I have much to learn and that I am really not adequate to the task. I agonize every week preparing . . . I sleep very badly on Saturday nights . . . and I have a ball in the pit of my stomach every Sunday until the end of the second service and I collapse at home." (A United Methodist Local Pastor)

It's called the Imposter Syndrome, the feeling of being unworthy of such a high calling, and it can be a wretched thing to experience. Your inner demon whispers that you don't know enough about the Bible, your spiritual life is a mess, your voice is squeaky—the reasons are legion and deeply personal. One student discovered the sermons of Barbara Brown Taylor and then almost refused to preach because she just knew she couldn't do it as well. Martin Luther aptly summed up the dread:

> I would rather be stretched upon a wheel or carry stones than preach one sermon. For anyone who is in this office will always be plagued, and therefore I have often said that the damned devil

and not a good man should be a preacher. But we're stuck with it
now. ("Sermon on the Twelfth Sunday after Trinity, 1531.")

We all have our inner demons and times that we feel unworthy to preach. If you are afraid, at least you are not alone. In
fact, my experience is that new preachers who feel as Luther did
turn out to be much better preachers than those who can't wait
to climb into the pulpit because they grasp the significance of
the calling and responsibility of the task. It is a good and biblical thing to be a reluctant prophet. But think carefully about
what exactly it is that makes you reluctant. Your inner reluctances are matters you must pray over and work through. For
some people, such reluctances turn out to be indications that
they really do not belong in the pulpit. For others, they are signs
of unrealistic images that they have about preachers, or some
burden of self-criticism from which they must be healed. For
still others, however, the sense of unworthiness comes from
years of being told that the pulpit is a place reserved only for
folks who are of a different gender, race, age, physical ability,
class, or educational background than theirs. Even if you are
never told explicitly that "people like you" should not preach, it
may be that you have simply never seen a person like yourself in
the pulpit and so have implicitly assumed that your voice was
not welcomed. Here we are up against not just our inner
demons, but against powers and principalities like racism,
ableism, sexism, and homophobia that plague the history of the
church. In this small book I cannot deal with all of these preju-
dices in relation to preaching other than to say that I believe
that the Spirit is moving through the church to continue to
break down the barriers that keep us from living fully and faithfully.

Yet because this is a book especially for new preachers, there
are two groups I wish to address directly, folks who have often
been barred from the pulpit: women and laity.

Women in the Pulpit

It is astounding that the birth of the church at Pentecost was marked by the promise that the Spirit would move both sons and daughters to prophesy (Acts 2:17; Joel 2:28-29), and yet the church has resisted the Spirit's gift to women ever since. If you are a woman moving from the pew to the pulpit, you may experience a deep reluctance to preach that men will never know. Because for so many centuries women were forbidden to preach (and still are in many denominations), you may sense that your voice is less expected and welcome or carries less weight than that of men. Despite the fact that women make up 61 percent of all U.S. worshipers and more than one third of the students in seminaries, only about 12 percent of all U.S. clergy are women. In most denominations, we are only one or two generations removed from the pioneering women who were first ordained. In other places women have been only reluctantly received, if at all.

The resistances are profound. You may encounter folks who will compliment your preaching, but then say offhandedly, "You preach well, but I just can't get used to the sound of a woman preacher." You may be paid less for your efforts than men. You may be bumped off the schedule or given second billing or slighted in an introduction if you share a service with a man. Even if there are no remaining sexist attitudes in your congregation there can be other obstacles: the pulpit may be too tall or the sound system tuned for lower voices, the prayers and hymns still talk about "men" rather than "men and women," or just plain "people." God is addressed as Almighty Father so many times in our prayers that it seems like we believe this is God's official and only name. No wonder some of the women students I encounter confess that they face an inner struggle about whether they have a right to stand in the pulpit! In both subtle and explicit ways, even in liberal churches women are sent the message that they really don't belong.

Women can be ambivalent about preaching even when they

are asked to do it precisely because the preaching office too often has been used to perpetuate patterns of authoritarianism. Refusing to stand towering over the gathered community, women will often leave the pulpit entirely and stand on the same level as the congregation, engaging it in a sermon that feels more like a dialogue among equals. This is what happens in the church to which I belong. At the time of the homily our female priest comes right up to the front pew to talk with us. The old oak pulpit stands against the wall on the left, used only by the occasional guest (usually male) preacher. It towers over us like an abandoned monument to an earlier style of preaching, of being church. The congregation beams because the preacher doesn't use it, yet any suggestion that it be removed will be greeted with a gasp of horror. Church furniture is often more sacred than God. (Don't believe me? Try moving the furniture around one week and see what happens.)

The good news is that the increase in women preachers is changing the nature of preaching in our day. Women embody sermons in ways that are often different from men. Many are rejecting universal claims in favor of more personal stories of faith, theological abstractions for testimonies of faith, moral simplicities for a more complex realization of what it means to try to live faithfully in our age. They are exploring biblical storytelling sermons, dialogue sermons, sermons-in-the-round, and other imaginative and inclusive forms of proclamation. Others use familiar patterns of preaching but embody them in new ways. Long story short: the church has suffered too long from hearing from only one-half of the human perspective. We are in continuing need of women who are willing to answer the call to move from pew to pulpit.

Lay Preachers

Ordination, traditionally, is the way churches have recognized the calling of particular people to ministries of Word, Sacrament, and Order. It is the way that life in the church normally runs.

Trouble is, God doesn't always seem to stick to what is normal. The history of the church shows again and again that the revival of lay preaching can bring renewal to the church.

- In Jewish synagogues, any layman could speak and give instruction (see Luke 4:16ff, and Acts 13:15). Thus, none of the apostles, nor Jesus himself, was formally ordained, yet they were welcome to speak in the synagogues.
- In the Middle Ages, although preaching at a Mass was reserved for priests and authorized monks, an unordained abbess was allowed to address her community.
- In the thirteenth century, first Dominic, and then Francis of Assisi, started new orders of monks who, despite being ordained, evangelized Europe with their learning, preaching, and exemplary lives.
- In Holland, there were so few preachers during the Reformation that a "school for prophets" was created for the laity, leading to the founding of the University of Leyden.
- Lay preaching revived strongly in the English-speaking world with the early Puritans and with the Quakers, who eagerly accepted both female and male lay preachers and sent them all over the world as evangelists and missionaries.
- The Methodist revival in Great Britain in the 1700s was almost entirely led by lay preachers, both men and women, who traveled from town to town preaching in fields and organizing class meetings.
- The Presbyterians in Scotland saw a revival of lay preaching in the 1800s, which in turn influenced the Anglican Church to establish the office of lay reader, a person authorized to preach and lead services in local parishes.

"Give me one hundred preachers who fear nothing but sin, and desire nothing but God, and I care not a straw whether they be clergymen or laymen; such alone will shake the gates of hell, and set up the Kingdom of God upon earth." (John Wesley)

Today, lay preachers across the world and across traditions serve small churches, supplement the preaching ministry of larger congregations, lead retreats and youth groups, and act as evangelists in some of the fastest growing congregations and church movements in the world. Informally, laity are invited to give testimonies, preach during special prayer services and revivals, fill in on Sundays when pastors are away, or simply preach whenever they are deemed to have something important to say in the life of the church. In our local congregation, for example, our pastor has asked one lay member to speak about how his faith sustains his work as an environmental activist; another to represent to the congregation the aspirations of the Native American people who live in the community. Most pastors are thrilled to get a break from the cycle of sermon preparation, and most congregations glad to hear from someone else for a change.

> "I began preaching in the 70s. . . . Actually it was lay witnessing. My 'born again' experience had been quite extraordinary and I felt moved by the Holy Spirit to testify one summer Sunday when the pastor was on vacation."   (A United Methodist Lay Pastor)

More formally, laypersons in various denominations are called, trained, and sent out specifically to take on the ministry of preaching in the local congregation and beyond. Unordained college and seminary students are given the responsibility of pastoral care and preaching in local churches overseen by more experienced, ordained persons. Many of the local churches in rural areas across America would simply close if all the unordained students who served them were barred from the pulpit. Most of my students leave seminary with two or three years of preaching experience under their belts, all of it gained before ordination.

Speaking about the good news of Jesus Christ is a task to which we are all called through our baptism. Scripture affirms:

"Let the word of Christ dwell in you richly; teach and admonish one another in all wisdom" (Colossians 3:16). Martin Luther thought that nothing mattered more than preaching because it led people to Christ. So important, in fact, that it could not be owned by the ordained: "The only true, genuine office of preaching, like priesthood and sacrifice, is common to all Christians." But, he added, for the sake of good order, "Not many of you are to preach at the same time, although all have the power to do it." This dual sense of both the need for lay preaching and the preservation of the good order of the church is present in most of our denominations. Most try to be faithful to scripture by both encouraging it and making sure that those who do it are adequately trained. For information about how different denominations name and train lay preachers, check out this book's Web site: www.pewtopulpit.com.

CHAPTER 2

Preaching with Others

Miguel was trained to preach at seminary and among Anglo congregations. When he became the pastor in a small urban church of Cuban émigrés, things changed:

"When I preached in Anglo congregations I wrote out my whole sermon, I took the manuscript, and then my world changed with this other congregation. Preaching is a more familiar, community-oriented event in the Latino congregation. I have to be closer to them, there needs to be more eye contact. The people I serve are mostly older immigrants with health problems. The first thing I did as a literate middle-class educated person was to tell them to open their Bibles and read. But I learned it has to be like my grandmother used to do, with storytelling. I began to be like Grandma, just telling stories from the Gospels that I would relate to our own stories. For example, every time something comes up like a mustard seed, or good seed versus weeds, they know the old agricultural images as children who grew up in Cuba. Since changing my preaching they have become more receptive and more active. What I have learned from that is the power of the spoken word."

The old paradigm of preaching viewed the preacher as a lone ranger, a solitary figure hunched over desk preparing a sermon. Like Tolkien's character, Gollum, who came to fixate on the ring as "my precious," the preacher considered the sermon something to protect until the time on Sunday that it was revealed to all. But there are many reasons today for the preacher to think of herself or himself as a member of a fellowship, a group of faithful persons on a long and sacred journey, and the sermon as a lens by which that fellowship can view the world that week as a God-soaked world.

You preach within a local community of faith. Sermons are shared experiences within the context of worship. Congregations are increasingly resisting the idea that Sunday morning ministry is something that is delivered to them. Thriving churches involve people in ministries within and beyond the local church, and these ministries become celebrated during Sunday worship. Active church members have a plethora of study resources available to them through Christian bookstores and the Internet and are looking for ways to share what they know. They have visited other congregations where they have seen worship that involves more people and they bring those expectations back to their home churches. The better pastors, for their part, are learning that their sermons remain fresher and are better heard if they involve others in the congregation as they prepare for and deliver their sermons.

You preach with a community of fellow preachers. Two recent developments, in particular, have encouraged preachers to work together as members of a community of preachers: the common lectionary and the growth of the Internet. Today church visitors to a small town with a United Methodist church on one corner, a Presbyterian one across the street, and a Congregationalist one on the other side of the intersection may find that they are all using the exact same scripture readings in worship on a Sunday morning. Pretty soon the preachers figure out that they might well benefit from trading ideas and resources rather than doing a solo act, or they may even do an occasional pulpit exchange or a community-wide worship service. With the Internet, these working groups lose their limitations of distance. Communities of preachers from all over the world now meet easily over the Internet to share sermons and tips about Bible lectionary texts.

IDEAS TO INCREASE THE COMMUNAL NATURE OF YOUR PREACHING

- Form and attend Bible study groups that meet the week before to consider the upcoming Sunday readings.
- Encourage the use of Sunday school materials that are tied to the lectionary. Participate in the discussion.
- Ask children what they think about a Bible story and let their responses guide your sermon preparation.
- Start a sermon feedback group to meet immediately after church to discuss a sermon.
- Read classic and contemporary sermons by other preachers, especially those from communities different from your own.
- Meet together with other preachers of your own denomination, or from different denominations, to study and share notes and ideas.
- Frequent Web sites that allow preachers to post illustrations, sermon ideas, and even whole sermons (but don't plagiarize).
- Develop and preach dialogue sermons with other members of the congregation.
- Get to know the people in the congregation well. Visit their homes and workplaces and find out what they care about.
- Make sure plenty of people are involved in planning and conducting the worship service.
- Be aware of community events, of movies that are engaging members of your congregation, of thresholds of life that members are encountering and crossing, and weave these experiences into your sermons.

You preach within the community of saints. The sermon takes place in the church, which of course is not a building, nor even a congregation, but one local gathering of a community of faithful memory that stretches over time and place. The purpose of the church and its preaching is to hold on to and be moved by the lively memories of the past, present, and future. As you think about the congregation with whom you will preach, picture

Abraham and Sarah laughing together just to be with all their children in faith, Mary and Joseph singing their amazement at what has come to pass through their child, and Saint Francis and Saint Clare of Assisi patiently waiting for the church to practice what it preaches. Indeed, no matter how many or few are physically present to hear your sermon, always know that you are also surrounded by the "great cloud of witnesses" (Hebrews 12:1) eager to hear what you have to say.

Trust Your Pew Experience

Trust your experiences as a hearer of sermons. They will be valuable to you as a preacher. The journey from the pew to pulpit may only be a few steps in the sanctuary, but it can be miles in your mind, and in the throes of anxiety about taking that journey you can easily forget to trust all that you already know. You know from hearing sermons what stories move the heart to praise and what ones feel flat or clichéd, what kind of humor helps and what kind is off-putting, what gestures are inviting and which are distracting. You've presumably heard your share of the good and the bad, and have gained some valuable insights into what makes one sermon soar and what makes another fall on the ground with a thump and die a slow and painful death.

People who have just started preaching often tell me that it ruined them as listeners: they will never again be able to hear a sermon naively, without analyzing its content, form, and delivery. Usually they say it with a sigh, as if remembering the day they found out about Santa Claus, keenly aware that the transition from pew to pulpit is spiritually significant for them, maybe even a loss to grieve.

Whether a gain or a loss, you will experience sermons differently once you start giving them. So take some time and write down what you already know about what makes a sermon effective or ineffective. Keep that list with you in the next few weeks in which you hear other sermons preached and develop the list further. Refer to those insights when you are knee-deep in sermon preparation yourself, or when you begin to doubt that you know what you are doing.

Remember How You Remember Sermons Yourself

When I ask people what makes a sermon good or effective, opinions fly. People seem to have no problem speaking in general about how they experience preaching. But then I ask a follow-up question: Can you remember a specific sermon that had a big impact on you? Without fail the room falls silent. In one workshop, after about thirty seconds of quiet thinking, a woman volunteered, "Well, I can tell you about a particular sermon that made me cringe." The rest of the room nodded as if to say that was their experience, too. "It was a sermon that drew from too many different traditions," she continued, "it had too much information in it, and I wasn't clear about what Christians should think." Another said she was turned off by a sermon on youth suicide that made her feel uncomfortable. It seemed that the preacher was using the sermon as a therapy session, and seemed to be doing his personal processing out loud.

Finally, when pressed for a positive example, someone else said he remembered a sermon from a Baptist pastor with memorable line: "A willingness to be at ease in Zion has no place in the life of the Christian." That sermon, he said, painted an image that had stayed with him for a long time. Then another person recalled a story sermon; and another, one that ended with a question.

What they do recall are impressions, stories, and feelings of being inspired or bored. Eventually, most of us can recall a few details of specific sermons, but it is striking how slowly those particular memories come. Then I realize that I'm not that different, even though I spend much of my life listening to and thinking about preaching. What I remember are the unusual sermons: one that explored a single word; another in which the preacher knocked over her glass of water; and one that mostly contained tips on how to juggle church parking for the crowded Christmas Eve services.

Then, more slowly, come felt images of sermons that had a deeper impact: a sermon by a student about how he experienced the life of faith the way Alexander the Great must have done when he marched his armies off the map of the known universe. That one is stuck forever in my memory because that student died a week later in a car accident, and I couldn't shake the idea of his own life marching off the map, or the sense of his young family exploring the barren landscape of grief.

A few individual sermons are memorable, but many more seem to get knit unremarkably into the fabric of our lives or get lost in the fog. Maybe this is a mark of a huge failure in contemporary preaching. If the sermon were richer in images, more demanding in content, more exciting in delivery, would it perhaps make a stronger impact on our memories, and like the new blockbuster at the megaplex be something that people talk about the next day? Or maybe that's the way sermons used to be when preachers painted the details of the fiery tortures of hell.

There is probably some truth in that. Psychologists know that the human brain "tags" events and memories that evoke strong emotions in us. These are the memories that are most likely to be stored for the long term and have the biggest impact on how we live our lives. Mostly likely, if you can remember a sermon that you heard a year ago or more it is because it created or evoked an intense emotional experience in you. Should preaching therefore seek to move the emotions? I believe so, although clearly the objective is not just to whip up emotion but to invite people to change their lives as a result of the powerful invitation of God.

By recalling how we remember sermons we learn first, that most of the individual sermons we will preach probably won't evoke strong enough memories to be recalled and acted upon in the long run. Second, we usually don't remember the details of even the most powerful sermons that we hear. Therefore, don't be disappointed when your congregation doesn't recall your intricate and much-studied explanation of the Twelve Tribes of Israel. Aim rather that your preaching will have a cumulative effect on the faithfulness of your hearers. Trying to change or convert them all at once can be manipulative, and conversion is really God's business anyway. In every sermon, be faithful to your topic, your text, and your people. Be passionate; try to change our hearts and minds, but give the Spirit room to move in each of us as we have need. The Golden Rule applies: preach to others as you would have them preach to you.

Being Yourself

I asked a small group of lay preachers in a workshop, "What is your biggest concern about preaching?" One of them said with a chuckle, "How can I preach in my own congregation where people know what a jerk I am?"

Although we laughed with him we also knew what he meant. When you stand in front of a congregation to preach you may suddenly become keenly aware of the familiar faces looking back at you. Especially in a small church you preach not with a blank slate but with a web of relationships that already exist and in which you may be a well-known strand. You are about to launch into a sermon about "loving your neighbor," when you glance to your left and there sits Jim, third row back near the aisle. He is a best friend of the mechanic who botched your car repair last month and made you so angry that you said a few choice words as you stormed out of his shop. Does Jim know about that? Or the sermon subject happens to be Matthew 25, where the Son of Man separates the sheep from the goats based on whether they fed the hungry, welcomed the stranger, visited those in prison, and took care of the sick. A few rows back is the Martos family. Their son has been in the hospital getting chemotherapy treatments and you realize that you have not called, sent a card, or brought them a meal as you had intended. We may fantasize about preaching or hearing preaching in a "relationally neutral" context, but to do so regularly would miss the deeper possibilities of preaching as two-way conversation about the most important questions and commitments in our lives.

> "Before I formed you in the womb I knew you,
> and before you were born I consecrated you;
> I appointed you a prophet to the nations."
>
> Then I said, "Ah, Lord GOD!
> Truly I do not know how to speak, for I am only a boy."
> But the LORD said to me,
> "Do not say, 'I am only a boy';
> for you shall go to all to whom I send you,
> and you shall speak whatever I command you." (Jeremiah 1:5-7)

In the book *Life Together*, Dietrich Bonhoeffer noted that genuine Christian community is only possible when we get out of our dream worlds and encounter one another as the true people we are: "Just as surely as God desires to lead us to a knowledge of genuine Christian fellowship, so surely must we be overwhelmed by a great disillusionment with others, with Christians in general, and, if we are fortunate, with ourselves."

What would it be like to preach a sermon on "love your neighbor" from the perspective of this "great disillusionment" with oneself and the church? It would not point fingers, but enter into an honest appraisal of just how hard it is to love another person as you love yourself. It might ask the same question that the lawyer asked of Jesus, "Who is my neighbor?" from the perspective of the refugees or migrant farm workers in your town. By imagining yourself, therefore, not in the position of Jesus giving the new commandment, but in the place of the rich young man for whom the cost of love is just too high, your sermon makes clear to Jim and the Martos family that you are a fellow disciple of Jesus, not a lawgiver from on high and a hypocrite. It explores in this time and in your specific community what it means to love your neighbor.

So think of preaching not as drawing anonymous graffiti with your finger in wet concrete, as wisdom for the ages. Rather, think of it as allowing yourself the freedom to respond to the movement of the Spirit, vibrating enough to be felt by the others on the web, but not so much as to be torn away from it. Let your sermon express deep regard for your hearers, and your sense that you are a part of them, not apart from them. Certainly never be haranguing or judgmental in tone. One of John Wesley's worst preaching moments had to be when, frustrated at the lack of religious ardor among the Methodists in Frederica, Georgia, he told them, "My poor friends, you are the scum of the earth!" Afterwards, Wesley noted that "some of the hearers were profited, and the rest deeply offended." He didn't preach there long.

Risking Yourself

If we take seriously the notion of the sermon as the invitation to a table of faith conversation, then we have to be willing to offer something worth chewing on. But it is disingenuous to open a conversation to which we are close-minded ourselves. It is repulsive only to offer food that is pre-chewed. A good sermon will risk a stance without painting people into corners. It will testify to how the preacher sees God working in the world, but not offer formulas for pinning God down. There is risk-taking with the hearers as well, who will have to decide what to do with your wager of faith or this new way of seeing the world.

A lay member of a local church in New Brunswick offered to speak to a small circle of church members who were talking about the meaning of Christ for them: "If I told you what I really believed you'd kick me out of the church." But simply saying this gave other people in the group permission to speak freely too about their personal convictions. Sometimes the best thing a sermon can do is testify to the questions we have, or point to mysteries we don't understand. What a gift a sermon can be when it refuses to give sure answers, but names the hard questions and lets us chew on them for a while as people of faith! The fear is that such radical honesty will somehow destroy the church by unhinging it from its traditional doctrines, but in actuality it creates church because it takes faith seriously as something that mature, thinking people do.

Being More than Yourself

"For we do not preach ourselves, but Jesus Christ as Lord, and ourselves as your servants for Jesus' sake."

(2 Corinthians 4:5 CEV)

The well-known preacher and theologian William H. Willimon commented in his book *Pastor* that in preaching, "it is not my task primarily to 'share myself' with my people, certainly not to heed the advice of those who say, 'Just be yourself.' As Mark Twain said, about the worst advice one can give anybody is, 'Just be yourself.' " Willimon stands in a long tradition of preaching among Protestants that believes preachers should get themselves out of the way of the Word of God. Their interpretation of Paul here is that the goal of preaching is to be transparent to the gospel.

I've never fully agreed with this nor even understood it as an ideal. Paul's letters to the Corinthians show that he was always using himself to make his gospel message known: he boasted about his apostleship, he spoke of his love for the church, and he recounted stories of his sufferings for Christ. Paul didn't preach himself, but he used himself to preach. Likewise, preaching always involves your full *self*: the reality of your body, the timbre of your voice, the culture in which you were raised, the language that you speak, the experiences you have had, the questions you have, the books that you have read, the teachers under whose influence you have come, and the quality of your faith-walk. Does this mean that in a sermon you are to "preach yourself"? By no means. You know from your own experience as a hearer that preachers who spend too much time giving the details of their lives from the pulpit have missed the mark. Good preachers are fully in touch with the limits and gifts of their humanity, but their goal is to use those to point to the gospel. It may be bad advice, according to Twain, to just "be yourself," but how can you do otherwise? Over the long run your preparation and practice as a preacher will change the self that you bring to preaching, and you will be more than what you are now. Christians who believe that God transforms people through the gospel must affirm that through grace, we will all become more than ourselves.

But for now, simply learn to draw from the well of your personal experience of divine grace and give us your testimony of it. The First Letter of Peter advises, "Always be ready to make your defense to anyone who demands from you an accounting for the hope that is in you" (1 Peter 3:15). Congregations do not just want to know that God is out there somewhere working in an abstract way. They want to know how God is at work right here and now, starting with the life of the preacher. So what is your hope right now? What do you really believe about God, the human condition, the call of Christ in the church today? In what ways are you able to trace the paths of God's ongoing work in the world? What have you discovered by paying close attention to the community of hearers, the community of fellow preachers, and the community of saints? How you answer those questions will be the testimony you have to offer.

Note that the passage above says that you are responsible for being able to name "the hope that is in you." Not *the* answer for all people and all times; not all the answers to all the questions that are out there, not even the answer you may give in the future as your beliefs and convictions grow, but an accounting of the one thing that drives your life forward in the light of God here and now: your hope. And then comes the kicker: "yet do it with gentleness and reverence" (1 Peter 3:16). You can know your testimony is true when it is offered with love and respect for your hearers, reflects the loving regard of God for all people, and takes us all into a future where we become more than our present selves by grace.

CHAPTER 3

Choosing a Text or Subject

L et's say that you have been invited to preach in two weeks. It may be that you have been invited to preach about a particular issue. It is Youth Day, for example, and you have been asked by the pastor to give your view on what God is calling the congregation to do in ministry with the youth in your area. In this case, the sermon already has a purpose and your task is fairly well defined. But more likely, you have just been given a date to preach and little other guidance. Where do you start to know what you should preach? Should you pick a specific text to explore? Some idea about God that has been bugging you lately? Something about your community that you think needs to be addressed? Something in the news? The purpose of this chapter is to give you some guidance about how to begin when you don't know where to begin.

Should Preaching Always Come from the Bible?

Sermons have generally been divided into two types, **expository** and **topical**. Expository preaching takes its starting point from the scripture, usually a single text, using it as a lens by which the congregation views its current experience. The word comes from the Latin *exponere*, meaning to put on view or display. The preacher's goal is therefore primarily to display or uncover the original meaning of the text before it is then applied to the reality of the congregation. A topical sermon begins from the reality of the congregation (or world) before it moves to the Bible. Perhaps it starts with an intuition that God is calling the congregation to support a new food pantry in the community, or seek reconciliation about an internal conflict. Or maybe it begins with a question about zoning at the edge of an endangered wetlands, an item in the headlines: human cloning, spousal abuse, or terrorism. You move from the question to an honest search in the Bible for stories that seem similar to what you are going through, or words from a prophet, from Jesus, or Paul, that address the matter.

> "To have to speak from a particular text to a particular congregation in an actual situation is in itself a dangerous undertaking."
>
> (Karl Barth)

Done well, neither method of preaching is inherently more "biblical" than the other. What they share is a genuine desire to find out how God is still speaking to us about relevant matters through the text of the scriptures. When expository sermons go bad, it is usually because the preacher has uncovered some hidden meaning in a passage that has no clear application or relevance to the real life of the congregation. When topical sermons get off track it is usually because they seek scriptural "proof" for a position that the preacher already holds. In both cases the preacher is treating the Bible as a dead book rather than as a Living Word, an open and ongoing dialogue between God's intention for us and our attempts to articulate and live in faithful response.

Whether your starting point is a biblical text or something

that is happening in the world, your task as a preacher is to help us see what God is up to and what God may be saying. Nothing more, nothing less. And if you do this you will be performing the most biblical kind of preaching there is. For what is the Bible but a collection of writings by people who are testifying to what they understand God to be up to: through the history of Israel, through Jesus of Nazareth, and through the work of the Holy Spirit in the church?

So **what does make a sermon biblical?** I would answer this way. A sermon is faithful to the Bible if it takes it seriously, wrestling with it honestly as a testimony of a people who have wrestled with God. It allows the living Spirit to move in, through, around, and even against the text. It never confuses the words on the page with the God who is beyond the page. It sees itself as a being in community with others who also take the Scriptures seriously and is honest about what it understands and what it doesn't understand. It strives to open up the relationship between the text and the congregation rather than close it down with once-for-all interpretations. It knows that the Bible has been used for good and for ill in the world, for the liberation and oppression of God's people, so it is sensitive to ways people who are different from the preacher may read a passage. And, finally, its purpose is not to testify to the Bible, but to testify to the God revealed by the Bible.

That is not a neat, easy answer, but then again, we don't have a neat, easy set of scriptures—sixty-six books, two testaments, four Gospels, twelve minor prophets. What we have is a community of books written over many generations, each trying to express what it hears of God's voice in its own time. Christians believe that preaching continues this vital work of interpreting God's movements in our world, using the shape and clues of scripture to give us clues as to where to look. It is not primarily about what God did back then, but about the good news of what God is doing now.

Starting with Biblical Texts

The Lectionary

A **lectionary** is a list of readings from the Bible assigned to particular days. There are "daily lectionaries," that is, calendars of readings for weekdays, but for preaching we will mostly be concerned with the weekly, or Sunday, lectionary. The purposes of lectionaries are to coordinate the scripture readings with the church year, to make sure that congregations hear a wide range of biblical texts, and to encourage the sense that worship is something the body of Christ does together even though there are many different congregations spread throughout the world.

Lectionaries have become widely used in Protestant congregations because of the work of the ecumenical group, the Consultation on Common Texts (www.commontexts.org), which has over twenty different church bodies as members. In 1983, this group published the widely used "Common Lectionary," but because of perceived shortcomings on how it used the Old Testament and how it neglected Bible texts that featured women, it was revised and republished in 1992 as the **Revised Common Lectionary** or **RCL**. Today, most mainline Protestant churches in North America use this lectionary, and it is being adopted or adapted by churches across the globe, from Korea to Scotland. Even churches like the Evangelical Lutheran Church of America and the Episcopal Church that have slightly different lectionaries have also approved the RCL for use in their congregations.

The Sunday lectionary includes four readings or "lessons," most typically, a passage from the Old Testament, a Psalm, a reading from part of the New Testament, and a reading from a Gospel. During Easter season, a reading from Acts will often be substituted for the Old Testament lesson. The lectionary is arranged in a three-year cycle. Year A focuses on Gospel readings from Matthew, Year B on Mark, and Year C on Luke. This way a congregation that uses the lectionary regularly can gain a deep sense of the characteristic voice of each of the three Synoptic Gospels. John's Gospel is more scattershot, appearing especially often in the Easter season and in the summer of Year B. Some people find this to be a weakness in the lectionary system and fear it may lead congregations to devalue the unique message and chronology of John.

Be aware that the Revised Common Lectionary has two different sets of Old Testament readings for Sundays between Pentecost and Advent. In the first set of readings, the Old Testament lesson and the Psalm are closely related to the Gospel reading. In the second set of readings—the set preferred by most Protestant denominations—the Old Testament readings are "semi-continuous" with one another, and are not intended to relate thematically with the Gospel lesson. During these Sundays, a lectionary congregation will hear the great stories of Genesis, Exodus, Joshua, and Judges in Year A; about David and his descendants in Year B; and about Elijah, Elisha, and the minor prophets in Year C. If you are a guest or occasional preacher in a lectionary congregation during the summer months, it is crucial that you find out which series the congregation is following. If you are in charge of selecting the texts for the whole season, stick with one set or the other.

Preaching the Lectionary

If your church uses the lectionary, your job in knowing where to begin is made somewhat easier. The way most lectionary preachers begin is to sit down and read each passage of the lectionary carefully. You still have to determine on which text or texts in the lectionary your sermon will focus. Don't try to preach on too many texts or feel the need to deal with all the readings given by the lectionary for that day. Sermons that focus on more than one text easily become too complicated. Also, remember that in the RCL, the texts may not be arranged by theme anyway.

One of the benefits of using the lectionary is that there are abundant resources for preaching and worship that are keyed to it. There are scripture commentaries, magazines like *Lectionary Homiletics*, books of art and even of movies whose themes relate to the readings of the lectionary. For links to such resources see www.pewtopulpit.com. This outpouring of material can be of help to your preaching, but it can also hide some key weaknesses of using the lectionary exclusively for preaching.

The chief weakness is that the lectionary does not include the whole of the Bible. Preachers who only use the lectionary will never preach on Obadiah, Nahum, the Third Letter of John, or Jude. Despite the fact that the Song of Songs has been one of the best loved of all the books of the Bible by Christians, the lectionary only includes one reading from it—likewise from Ecclesiastes, 2 Chronicles, and Esther—and only two from Leviticus, Judges, and Ruth.

Another weakness is that because lectionary scriptures are tied to the liturgical season, preachers often find themselves explaining the meaning of the season of the year, rather than preaching the scriptures. Instead of designing a sermon and worship service that helps their congregations experience the expectation of advent and the joy of Easter, they subject them to sermons about how the season came about and why it is important—topics better covered in books and Sunday school classes than in sermons.

Finally, and most important, lectionary preachers can easily become irrelevant preachers. Let's say that it is Year B, the first week of July. The lectionary readings for that day include the account of David ascending the throne, a psalm that praises the beauty of Mount Zion, Paul's claim that he had an out-of-body experience, and Jesus sending the disciples out two by two. When you first read these lessons a week ago, you thought it might be a good idea to preach a sermon about how Jesus forms disciples by sending them on mission projects because the youth of the church are soon going on a trip to Appalachia. But during the week two of your youth are killed in a car accident or the city council voted to move the police station from its downtown location where it was a visible presence in a struggling neighborhood to a place out by the suburban mall accessible only by car. A sensitive pastor may find that the best thing to do is preach a sermon about grief and hope on the one hand, or on gospel engagement with politics on the other. Slaves of the lectionary may try to force the assigned scriptures to address topics that are not central to it, or, even worse, be so focused on the Bible texts that it doesn't even occur to them to preach on the pastoral needs of the present. In either case, there are times when even faithful lectionary preachers do well to understand the limitations as well as the gifts of the lectionary as they decide on what to preach.

Nonlectionary Biblical Preaching

If you are not a lectionary preacher, and if you will normally begin your sermon preparation from a Bible text rather than a topic, then you will choose a text based on your own reading of the Bible and the needs of your congregation. It was once common for preachers to pick a single verse or even a portion of a verse as the basis for their sermons. It is probably more faithful in the long run to consider larger portions of scripture for your sermons. Don't limit the reading of scripture in worship to the one or two verses on which you plan to preach. Read from the New and Old Testaments regularly and let the congregation participate in reading or singing psalms. It is one of the great ironies of contemporary American church life that the congregations that say they are most based in scripture often hear the smallest portion of scripture read in worship. Christians believe that God speaks through Scripture, whether or not a preacher is there to comment on it, so don't be stingy with the Bible in worship!

If you preach regularly, you will find it helpful to work ahead by at least a week or two so that you can pick preaching texts when you are in a relaxed and prayerful mood. Here are a few ideas for working ahead:

- Preach a sermon series. Give a series on the families of Genesis, the life and ministry of Elijah, the Exodus story, Job, the minor prophets, a trip through a Gospel, a letter of Paul, the relevance of Revelation, or the spiritual gifts.
- Pick up a scripture text that is being used in the Sunday school class or a vacation Bible school.
- Pick scriptures that go with the theme of the year: stories of the birth of Jesus at Christmastime, or resurrection stories at Easter.

It is clarifying for all preachers, both lectionary and nonlectionary, to do yearly audits of the texts and subjects they actually preach on. You may discover that you are preaching too often from Paul's letters and not enough from the Old Testament, or too often on John's Gospel, and not enough from the prophets. Likewise, you may discover that you preach messages of comfort too often and not enough of spiritual challenge, or too often on social/political issues and not enough about the individual spiritual life. Beware of falling into preaching ruts or using only those texts that you find most congenial to your point of view. Expand your repertoire and don't avoid hard or famous passages. Explore the forgotten corners of the Bible: find out what Obadiah has to say to us today, struggle with Lamentations, or look for insight from the Third Letter of John.

EXERCISE

Let's say you wish to preach a sermon to your congregation to encourage them to follow their dreams. What scripture text might you choose to back up that message? Why? Where would you go to look up Bible texts about dreams? Now, do the same exercise for a sermon whose purpose is to ask a congregation to support a missionary; or, for a sermon designed to resolve a church conflict.

No matter how high your regard for scripture, not every verse can be squeezed for meaning. The Bible is not a flat surface, but a rollicking tale of people who lived in relationship with God, with high points and low in their faith, a tale that sometimes seems as if God is not even in the picture (God is never mentioned in the book of Esther, for example). One of the more interesting kinds of biblical sermons is to put texts that seem to conflict with one another in a dialogue. For example, how do you make sense of Jesus telling his disciples at the arrest scene in Matthew (26:51-53) to "put your sword back into its place; for all who take the sword will perish by the sword;" when earlier in Matthew Jesus has told his disciples that "I have not come to bring peace, but a sword" (Matthew 10:34; and see also Luke 22:36!).

SOME INTERESTING WAYS TO PREACH THE BIBLE

- Give a character sketch
- Trace a theme in scripture
- Trace the life of a minor character in the Bible
- Compare two conflicting texts
- Retell a story using contemporary language and characters
- Talk back to a prophet
- Ask Jesus a difficult question
- Explore a psalm
- Preach verse by verse
- Preach on a single word in scripture
- Pick a text you don't understand and explain why you don't understand it
- Compare scriptures from the Old and New Testaments

Picking a Topic

I've said a lot about preaching from the Bible because it is the way that most preachers begin. However, we noticed that oftentimes sermons that begin in the Bible really end up being topical sermons. So now a word for preachers who want to develop a sermon based on a given topic. Where do you come up with ideas?

One tack is to treat the major themes of our faith: grace, sin, or stewardship. Preach on the topic of the Holy Spirit sometime, the hope of heaven, or the importance of communion and baptism. Give a series of sermons that instruct people in the basics of prayer. Talk about what it means to grow in the faith or to raise your children in faith. Preach on what it means to live in a community that includes Hindus, Muslims, and Buddhists as well as Christians.

GENERATING IDEAS FOR TOPICS

- Visit the workplaces of your congregation
- Pick a section of the Apostles' Creed
- Read the local news
- Watch popular films
- Go to a city council meeting
- Explore the meaning of a sacrament or a Christian holiday
- Visit other local churches, synagogues, and mosques
- Talk to people who don't believe the same way as you
- Go to the library and bookstores and look at the new books being published
- Listen closely for the difficulties that members of your congregation are experiencing and pray for them often

Good ideas come from good listeners, preachers who are good at noticing what is really going on around them. Listen to the questions and concerns of your congregation and community. Read the local newspaper, talk with the old-timers and the newcomers in your congregation. Pay attention to the decisions being wrestled with in your county or city government. It has been my experience that topical preachers often draw from the national news on which to base their sermons: news of terrorists, wars, famines, and disasters that tend to grab the headlines and hence our anxieties. In a way, sermons on these broader issues are easy to preach about precisely because they are so big. We can decry the injustice of a war or grieve a terrorist act, but leave the sermon hearer with little to do about it other than feel bad because the decisions are being made by people so far away.

But congregations exist in local communities, communities that have racial divisions, economic inequalities, and spouses being abused behind doors in quiet neighborhoods. A topical sermon about a local issue is both more important and more dangerous because it can more easily ask people to get up and do something as a result: protest the lack of minorities on a planning board, support a job-training initiative, or volunteer at a women's shelter.

Sometimes new preachers look ahead to a lifetime of preaching and wonder how they will ever think of that many things to say. Such fears are unfounded. If you pray often, read the Bible, and keep yourself informed then there will be no end of things to preach about. As the great Episcopal bishop and preacher, Phillips Brooks, once wrote: "Care not for your sermon, but for your truth, and for your people; and subjects will spring up on every side of you, and the chances to preach upon them will be all too few."

CHAPTER 4

Hearing the Bible Again for the First Time

The hardest thing to do when beginning to preach from the Bible is to read it—really read it. Here you are at the desk, the Bible is in front of you. The date of your upcoming sermon is looming on the calendar and in your mind. The anxiety of preparing to deliver the Word of God makes your brain flutter a little more quickly than it would if you were just reading the Bible for personal edification or in a study group. Your anxiety leads you to scan down the text looking for something yelling, "Preach me! Preach me!" But you discover that your text is from Luke 15, the prodigal son. Oh no! What on earth are you going to say new about this old story? You offer a panicky prayer: "Jesus, help me!" While I believe that God does guide the preacher toward passages and messages that are intended for a congregation, I don't believe that these magically appear to us, especially as answers to panicky prayers. There was a day in which some preachers practiced a form of bibliomancy: they would climb the pulpit, close their eyes, flip through the Bible, and plunk their finger on a verse. Wherever it landed, they reasoned, was the text that God wanted the congregation to hear that morning. Woe to the congregation whose pastor's finger landed on Ezekiel 32:5: "I will strew your flesh on the mountains, and fill the valleys with your carcass." No, magical thinking will not do to prepare us to preach and good preaching doesn't typically come from texts that "jump out" at you any more than it does from random finger pointing, however piously done.

Rather than bibliomancy or panicky prayers, better to take some time to develop the ordinary grace of learning to read the Bible carefully and thoughtfully and let the idea for the sermon slowly grow. Perhaps the most important piece of advice I have to give you for developing a sermon from a text is that at the first stage of preparation, do not think about your sermon at all. Take the knowledge that you are doing this work for the sake of a sermon and put it in brackets. If you prefer a meteorological metaphor, every time you begin to worry about your sermon, picture it as a cloud and let it float gently away.

Your task at this point is simply this: to read the text closely, and as if for the first time. Ask of it every conceivable question, explore it for your own benefit as a person of faith, and consider whether God is speaking to you in the text. Open yourself to a dialogue with the Bible, perhaps a closer conversation than you've ever had with it before, and pray, not for your sermon but for yourself. What you learn in your study for preaching may forever change your understanding of scripture. It may challenge your understanding of your church. It may deepen or lessen your ardor for your particular beliefs. I say "lessen" intentionally, because I believe that unless you are truly willing to risk some of your most closely held convictions in the process of sermon preparation you are not exercising faith. Unless you are simply going to utter platitudes from the pulpit or repeat to your congregation what you read somewhere in a book, prepare to wrestle as Jacob did at the Jabbok. That's the only way to get a blessing.

How important is this first deep reading for your sermon? Absolutely critical. This is the only time in the process that you will be in the same position as the hearers in the pews. From this point forward you will be encountering the text in more detail and at more leisure than your hearers will have. Your honest and leisurely dialogue with the Bible opens you up to receive the Spirit. Anxious concern about your sermon and too much eagerness to get it done or get the point of your sermon actually closes down the possibility that God may speak through you in surprising and new ways.

How to Read the Biblical Text

Here are some tips about how to hear the Bible as if for the first time.

- *Choose a good translation* (more about that later) *and find some extended time to yourself.*
- *Open your Bible to the text and have a pen and paper ready.* I prefer to have a book and paper before me, rather than reading the text from a computer screen or using a word processor to take notes at this stage, because I find it less distracting. The physical process of writing down your thoughts is an important part of the memory process that I don't find is duplicated by typing.
- *Read the passage(s) through once or twice and get the flow of it.* I strongly suggest that you read it aloud as the ancients did to better hear the pace of the words.
- *Pay attention to how the text makes you feel:* Intrigued? Peaceful? Agitated? Bored? For example, when you read Psalm 29's description of a God who makes oaks to whirl and "flashes forth flames of fire," do you feel awe? Or when you read in Ephesians 5:22, "Wives, be subject to your husbands as you are to the Lord" does it make you feel angry? Humbled? Confused?
- *Spend some time considering what memories the text evokes in you.* These don't have to be pious memories at all. For example, when I hear Jesus say to his disciples in John 14:2: "In my Father's house there are many dwelling places," I

remember two specific things, that this was a text read at my own father's funeral (which is a sad memory, of course), and I remember a small country restaurant at which I once ate in rural Ohio. It was apparently run by Christians because at each table were corny religious placemats with this verse printed on it and a row of Victorian houses on it sitting on clouds with angels all around. So when you first read the text, it's important not to pull any punches here, but to go to the most vivid memories you have whether positive or negative. Let's say that the text instead is from Abraham's offering of Isaac as a sacrifice. This text may evoke terrible memories of family violence in some people, or in others the memory of a near-death experience or a time when they were rescued from harm. These memories may never make it into the final sermon, but acknowledging their presence in your life is crucial to hearing the text honestly.

- *Jot down any images that come to mind from works of art, television shows, or ordinary life. Brainstorm.* When I think of "many dwelling places," I think of skyscrapers in New York City, or the small caves people have dug out for themselves in the soft rock of central Turkey, or busy purple martin houses full of birds, or the tarp-covered camps of homeless men and women who live in the woods near our interstate ramp.

- *Jot down all the factual questions that you can think of, no matter how obvious they might seem to you at first. Use the Five W's to guide you: Who, What, When, Where, Why:*

  ○ **Who** wrote this book? Who was Jonah? To whom is this epistle or book addressed?

  ○ **What** were ships like back then? What kind of fish swallowed him? How big was Nineveh? What are sackcloths? What does this story say about God?

  ○ **When** was this book written? When did these events supposedly occur? How does this story fit in the timeline of the rest of the Bible?

  ○ **Where** is Tarshish? Where is Nineveh? Can I trace the journey that Jonah took?

- **Why** was this story handed on? Why did Jonah run away? Why should I pay attention to it today?

  If you do this step well, you will easily generate a list of twenty or thirty questions. You will also have made yourself a good list of things to study later as you continue to prepare.

- *If your text is a story, think about the different characters in it.* Which ones are the major characters? The minor ones? Where else do they show up in the Bible? Can you imagine what the story would seem like from their different perspectives? Write these down.

- *Look at how the text seems to fit with the rest of the book that it is located in.* What role does it play in the development of the book or letter? For example, how does Nathan's rebuke of David in 2 Samuel 12:1-6 fit into the larger story of Bathsheba and what follows later in the story of David's reign? If you aren't sure, make a note of this for future study.

- *What does the text say about who God is? Who Jesus is? What the church is? What salvation means?* Write down these and other theological questions that the text evokes in you.

- *Step back from the text now and try to imagine what God might be saying to you through it.* What convictions it provokes in you about faith, life, others, and the world? Write all of these down.

- *Begin to play with the hearing of the text:* for what persons might this text represent good news? For what persons might it represent bad news? What difference does it make that you are reading the text through the eyes of your gender, class, race, social/political location, or sexual identity?

This process can take an hour or more and give you four or five pages of notes for every passage with which you spend time. Since I normally preach from the lectionary, it is not unusual for me to go through this entire exercise with two or three of the lessons. In the end I'll most likely discard all my notes except those I took on the passage on which I will eventually preach. That's life. This process takes time and it's good to learn a basic lesson about preaching now: you will cut out at least as much material as you eventually keep in the sermon.

An Example

It wouldn't be helpful to include my entire four pages of notes on a given text at this point. However you may be interested to see an example of the many kinds of questions that a text can evoke. This is a randomly chosen passage that shows some of the questions that can come up when you read the Bible closely. Look for Who, What, When, Where, and Why questions in the mix.

Matthew 17:24-27

When they (who are they, Peter, James, and John [as in 16:1], the disciples [as in 16:10 and 13] or the crowd ([as in 16:14]?) **reached Capernaum** (where is Capernaum on the map? Where else does it show up in the Bible? Where was this group traveling from?), **the collectors of the temple tax** (what is this tax? Who are the collectors? How much was the tax?) **came to Peter and said, "Does your teacher not pay the temple tax?"** (Why would they ask this? Had Jesus given them some indication that he was not planning to pay it? Was this a trap? Where else do people try to trap Jesus?) **He said, "Yes, he does." And when he** (who is "he"? Peter or Jesus?) **came home** (is Jesus' home in Capernaum?), **Jesus spoke of it first** (does this show that Jesus could read Peter's mind or miraculously knew this discussion had happened?), **asking, "What do you think, Simon?** (Is it significant that the names Simon and Peter are both used here?) **From whom do kings of the earth take toll or tribute? From their children or from others?"** **When Peter said, "From others," Jesus said to him,**

"Then the children are free. (What does this mean? Which children?) **However, so that we do not give offense to them** (who is "them?" the tax collectors?), **go to the sea** (which sea, Galilee?) **and cast a hook; take the first fish** (what kind of fish do they have there? What memories do I have of fishing? Any unusual fish stories come to mind?) **that comes up; and when you open its mouth, you will find a coin** (what were coins like back then? How can a fish with a coin in its mouth also bite a hook!?); **take that and give it to them for you and me."**

In addition, this short text would lead me to ask other questions like:

- What does the Old Testament say about a temple tax? Who paid it? What happened if you didn't pay it? Was it a popular or unpopular tax?
- What taxes do I have to pay? How are they collected? What happens if I don't pay them?
- Where does this story show up in the other three Gospels, or is it only in Matthew? Where else do "fish tales" appear in Matthew?
- What does Jesus' comment that the "children are free" really mean?
- What is the purpose of this text? To show Jesus as a miracle worker who can read minds and find fish with coins in their mouths? To show that Jesus was a faithful Jew who supported the temple?
- In the end, Jesus and Peter don't really pay the tax out of their own pockets. What does this mean, if anything?
- What might Peter be thinking about all of this?
- I notice that the story doesn't actually show Peter going to get a coin from a fish's mouth. Does this mean that it didn't actually happen, or that Jesus is being comical here? Is this a way of saying that he refuses to pay the tax?
- What kind of fish did they/do they have in the area? How big are they?

- Memories: my dad and I going fishing in Maine when I was a kid and catching all kinds of odd-looking creatures. Paying taxes this year was particularly painful because we owed so much.
- Images: I know that one of the common signs of Jesus is the fish, and there are all kinds of "Jesus fishes" on the back of cars these days. What about tax protesters, people who refuse to pay income taxes?
- Movie: The film *Big Fish* involves storytelling and the ultimate fish story.
- Stories: Aren't there some old folktales that involve people catching magical fish? A children's story of Henry Huggins and his dog Ribsy catching a huge fish together?

And so on.

This is a very brief text of just four verses and yet I've already gathered a good head of steam just by looking closely at it. I have a lot of things to find out about, from where to find Capernaum on the map to how to see if my hunch is correct that there are folk tales that involve a magical fish. Already I'm hip deep in thinking and study and I haven't even cracked a book yet or opened my Web browser. My curiosity has been aroused but I haven't jumped to any conclusions about what my sermon may eventually be about.

Letting It Steep

After finishing this close reading of the text, stop your sermon preparation and set it aside. If you have the luxury of time (that is, haven't waited until Saturday to prepare!), don't do anything else on the sermon for a day or so. Let your thoughts about the sermon ripen slowly. So, put your sermon on the back shelf of your mind and let it sit there like a can of preserves, gaining flavor with time. You may find, as many students have reported, that the Spirit will speak to you at some unexpected time when you are relaxed or thinking of something else. The morning shower seems to be a place of great insight for sermons, and more than once I have wrapped a towel around me and padded to my desk to jot down some fresh idea or approach.

EXERCISE

Take one or more of the following texts and do a close reading as described in this chapter.
- Exodus 10:12-20: The plague of locusts
- Psalm 133: In praise of unity
- Lamentations 1: the destruction of Jerusalem
- John 18:1-11: Jesus is arrested in the garden
- 2 Corinthians 6:14-18: Paul's injunction not to be "mismatched with unbelievers"

CHAPTER 5

Working Up to Your Sermon

Preaching and Study

I looked over my very first sermon recently, preached to a seminary classroom on Philippians 3:12 ("Not that I have already obtained this or have already reached the goal; but I press on to make it my own, because Christ Jesus has made me his own."). It revealed an apparent belief that if I parsed every Greek verb correctly and discovered the original intention of Saint Paul, then God-inspired scriptural meaning would flow from the books of scholars, off my tongue, and into the ears of the congregations, eagerly waiting to hear the latest thoughts on how best to translate the word *teleioo-* (to make perfect or complete).

You and I have heard this kind of preaching, and we both know better. Please don't misunderstand this to be a brand of anti-intellectualism. The churches would be lost without preachers who have the time, inclination, and ability to do the kind of advanced study of scriptures that congregation members don't have. The rest of this chapter is devoted to outlining a study method that will lead to good preaching, and it assumes that most of us do too little reading and study, not too much.

But it is important to remember that the Spirit remarkably

43

descends on people in many ways for preaching. When you dive deeply into the life of study, the goal is not to get lost down there among the oysters but to resurface with a pearl in your hand. Our best preachers discover that hard study is a gift, not a straitjacket for creativity.

Exegesis

Bible students use the word "exegesis" (to lead or interpret) to describe the critical explanation or interpretation of the biblical text. One goal of exegesis is simply to understand, as best one can, the original meaning of the text in its original context and community. In your conversation with the Bible, this is the time when the Bible speaks and you listen as closely and carefully as possible. Exegesis is only one step in preparing to preach from a text, however, because even if one understands what the text originally meant (and the proliferation of different commentaries proves that this is rarely certain), this does not automatically mean you understand how it applies to the context of your congregation. Preachers quickly learn that it is at least as important to "exegete" their congregation skillfully as it is to interpret the text.

The rest of the chapter is the method of studying for a sermon that I most often use and the one that I recommend to my students. It is similar to methods that you will find in other preaching books: ladder-like steps that lead us down to the firm ground of a solid sermon. Most of my students who follow these steps carefully find them helpful and end up with engaging and informed sermons. However, some resist this method and report that any step-by-step method is too logical, too left-brained for them. They follow a more organic, circular path, in which they move back and forth between the different stations mentioned here. Study, conversation, dreaming, writing, and rewriting weave together in ways they don't entirely understand, but come Sunday they have a beautiful and faithful sermon to offer. So let's just say that what I offer you here are stations that you should visit as you prepare the sermon. I recommend that new preach-ers follow them in order, but most important is that you not miss any along the way.

Picking Up Where You Left Off

I hope you have taken a break from your study of the biblical text for Sunday and are starting again feeling refreshed. This means that you will need to remind yourself of the text and your notes by rereading them. If you sat with and studied your text as described in the previous chapter, you will have several pages of notes before you. You've got questions aplenty already and a full plate of things to investigate. But there are yet a few more dishes in the buffet line that you will want to sample before you really sit down to eat.

THE PREACHER'S MOST INDISPENSABLE TOOL: THE STUDY BIBLE

A good study Bible is the most indispensable tool for newcomers to preaching. Most have features such as interpretive notes, maps, genealogies, comments, cross-references, and indices. Many excel-lent sermons can arise primarily from sustained and careful use of a study Bible to pursue the questions you have already discovered about your preaching text. Yet with dozens of English translations available in countless editions, it helps to stop and think before going to the local bookstore or your favorite Web merchant and spending your money. For information about different Bible transla-tions, the different editions they come in, and how to pick a good study Bible for preaching, go to www.pewtopulpit.com.

Check the Footnotes

In any good study Bible you will notice many footnotes along the sides or bottoms of the pages. Sometimes these notes refer you to other portions of scripture that say similar things. Be sure to check those out and add them to your own notes. For example, if you are scheduled to preach on 1 Corinthians 11:23-25, Paul's passage about the institution of the Lord's Supper, you will also want to compare this account with those given by Matthew 26:26-30; Mark 14:22-26; and Luke 22:14-22. One thing you'll notice is that Matthew and Mark have Jesus "blessing" the bread, while 1 Corinthians and Luke say that he gave thanks over it. A significant difference, or not? You decide. More telling, perhaps, is that Luke mentions Jesus giving thanks over two cups (!), one at the beginning of the meal and one at the end. Now here is something worth investigation.

Other footnotes suggest that the Greek or Hebrew say something slightly different from the translation. In the passage we were considering earlier from Matthew 17:24-27, the footnote in the *New Oxford Annotated Bible* says that the original Greek calls the temple tax the *didrachma*, and the coin in the fish's mouth a *stater* that is worth two *didrachmas*. The plot thickens! Here are two more things to investigate.

Sometimes the footnotes give a different rendering of the meaning of the text. In the Learning Bible (CEV), for example, a footnote for Ephesians 5:14, "Light shows up everything," suggests that it may also be translated as, "Everything that is seen in the light becomes light itself."

Look also for footnotes that show that the early manuscripts may disagree with one another. The New Testament, especially, is based on fragments of many early editions that are often quite different from one another. Mistakes slipped in when the manuscripts were copied, and different regions sometimes had slightly different versions circulating. The result is that it has been a huge scholarly undertaking to try to discover what were the "original" versions of the biblical texts.

Sometimes these variations are quite significant. For example, Paul's command that "women should be silent in the churches" in 1 Corinthians 14:34-35 is not included in many early versions of this letter. It may have been added later by an editor. Earlier in Matthew 17, a footnote in the *New Oxford Annotated Bible* guides the reader to the discovery that "Other ancient authorities add verse 21: *But this kind does not come out except by prayer and fasting.*" The translators of the NRSV have studied the ancient manuscript evidence and decided that the earliest and best editions of the text did not include that verse. But how differently the passage sounds for preaching with verse 21 included or excluded. Jesus seems to be saying that it takes more than just faith to get rid of some demons; it takes strong spiritual disciplines as well.

The more closely you read the Bible, the more you will notice these variations. It shows us, again, that the scriptures were not magically beamed to the earth by God, but given through people of faith and passed down by copyists and publishers who sometimes changed the text along the way.

Read Around Your Text

If you have chosen your own preaching text, you already know that your choice has been somewhat arbitrary. You could have made it longer or shorter, started here rather than there. All choices about scripture texts for preaching are *choices* made by you or by a lectionary committee. These choices are not sacred. As far as I know God has never said, "Thou shalt preach only from John 1:1-14, stopping the reading before you get too far into the story of John the Baptist." The readings or lections are at best good guesses about what strings of words might best hang together for reading in church. Sometimes sentences or passages are left out. For example, the Revised Common Lectionary for the Sunday between November 6 and November 12, Year A, has Joshua 24:1-3a, 14-25 listed as the Old Testament lesson. It omits 3b-13, a long segment of Joshua's speech to the assembled tribes of Israel in which he recounts the faithfulness of the Lord. Verse 14's command to revere the Lord and put away idols is really meant to be a response to the Lord's faithfulness, a meaning that is lost if you only read the lectionary text as given.

Some lectionary dates give you choices. For example, in the RCL for the Second Sunday after Christmas, the Gospel lesson is John 1:10-18; but it gives you the choice of including 1:1-9, the opening words from John. What choice you make about whether to use the entire reading in church can make a big difference in how you preach the text.

For all texts, look at the context of the text. What difference does it make to begin and end the text at a certain place? What choices have been made by the lectionary editors? For example: 1 Peter 2:19-25 (a lectionary reading for 4 Easter, Year A) sounds at first like an encouragement to all Christians undergoing suffering: "For it is a credit to you if, being aware of God, you endure pain while suffering unjustly" (19). However, by backing up one more verse to verse 18, it becomes clear that this advice is being given specifically to slaves, who are being told to "accept the authority of your masters." And suddenly what sounds like advice to all suffering Christians becomes a more complicated passage to preach on given American Christianity's troubled history on the issue of slavery.

As they say in the real estate business: location, location, location. You simply can't understand a given passage outside of its location or context in the book or letter as a whole. So read around the passage, at least two chapters before and two chapters after your chosen text. Find out how the text fits into the overall argument of a letter, or the larger story related in the scripture. Good study Bibles, again, will often include outlines of the book you are reading to give you more insight on this. Write down anything you discover about the context of the text.

If you have done this work well, you have spent another good hour or more on your text. Your notes continue to multiply and you are wondering whether any of this will ever lead to a sermon. Trust the process. You are becoming a good student of your text, swimming around the oyster bed and finding pearls. But now it is time to surface and take another breath. I recommend this as an appropriate place to stop again and let your work simmer.

Study the Text

During the next session of sermon preparation you will follow the leads that you have uncovered. Up until this point you haven't cracked a book other than your study Bible. However, you have become so thoroughly familiar with the text that when you do open up dictionaries, concordances, and commentaries, you do so as an informed student, not a desperate seeker looking for wisdom to drop on you from on high. I recommend still that you *do not yet read commentaries* until you have progressed well into your research. Your sermon preparation will feel more alive for you if you continue to explore the specific questions you have rather than start to read overviews by other students of your text.

Take your questions and insights one by one and explore them more deeply. You can study particular words using a concordance, dictionary, or encyclopedia, do character studies of the people who are mentioned, find out more about who wrote the letter or book you are reading and why. You can't come to an exhaustive knowledge of your passage in studying for one sermon, so follow your interests and see where they take you. There are, however, four central areas you should touch on before you can consider your study complete. I'll describe each of these and then give examples of how they might apply to the text I've been exploring from Matthew. In the process, I will refer to a number of Bible study resources with which you may not be familiar, like interlinear Bibles and concordances. You can find explanations and examples of these on the Web at www.pewtopulpit.com.

1. The background of the text

Your study should give you a deeper awareness of the culture from which the text emerged. If you have asked good When, What, Where, Who, and Why questions, then you can't help learning more about the text's background as you work to find answers to them. Here are some questions to consider: What is the history behind your scripture? When did it get written, by whom, and why? If your text is retelling or alluding to the history of Israel, Jesus, or the early church, how much earlier did the event in the scripture occur before it was written down? Was your text written by a single voice or is it a weaving of the perspectives of different writers? With what aspects of daily life does it assume the reader is acquainted? To find out these things you can go to Bible atlases, dictionaries, and encyclopedias, introductions to the book of the Bible in your study Bible and do searches on the Internet.

Here are just a few examples of how I applied some of the questions I raised in my study of Matthew 17:24-27 to learn more about the background of the text:

- What was the temple tax? I discover from a Bible dictionary that it was called the *"didrachma,"* a half-shekel tax paid by loyal Jews over twenty and that it derives originally from Nehemiah 10:32-33 and Exodus 30:11-16. I learn about the role of tax collectors along the way and that by Jesus' day this was a much-disputed tax.

- Where is Capernaum? I look on a map or Bible atlas and locate Capernaum on the north shore of the Sea of Galilee. I find out using a concordance that Capernaum is mentioned four times in Matthew and sixteen times in the Gospels, but nowhere else in the New Testament. I read those passages and find out that many healing and teaching stories occurred in Capernaum and that it may have been the adult Jesus' home, as well as the hometown of Peter and Andrew. A look in a Bible dictionary entry for Capernaum yields pictures, scripture references, and information about the synagogue there.

- What kind of fish did they catch and eat? I learn from a Bible dictionary that one of the most common fish in that region is the Tilapia. Once I know this, I look up "Tilapia" on the Internet and find out how big they are, where they live, and even how to cook them.

2. The literary qualities of the text

The Biblical Context

Make sure that you take the time to learn more about the context of the biblical text and how it fits in with the rest of the Bible. Are there similar stories elsewhere? Does the New Testament text allude to something in the Old? Do the characters show up elsewhere? If you are studying a Gospel text, look in a parallel Gospels book to find out whether a version of it also appears in any of the other three Gospels and what the differences are.

Word Studies

Are there particular words that stand out as significant? You will want to look those up in a concordance or lexicon.

Form

What kind of text do you have: a story, a dictate of religious law, a song, poem, parable, letter, or prophecy? And what kind of effect do you think this text was meant to have on its hearers? Every genre has its own genius and way of rendering meaning, just as today we understand instant messages, a newscast, and a magazine article each specialize in communicating specific kinds of information well. In a similar way, biblical histories are meant to highlight God's presence and role in the story of Israel and the early church, psalms are meant to raise voices in praise and prayer and lament, epistles are often addressed to specific congregations and issues, and Gospels are written to give a particular meaning to the story of Jesus. It will help you to understand your passage if you consider how the form of the text gives clues as to its original purpose.

Structure

Remember that much of the Bible was written to be read aloud to listeners who were adept at identifying common themes, character developments, and plot twists. Get a sense of this by reading aloud and writing down your own outline of the flow of the text and how it unfolds. Does it repeat itself? Where is the climax or turning point?

Here are a few examples of how I explored the literary qualities of Matthew 17:24-27:

- Using a concordance, I discover that there are seven other passages in which the word "fish" is mentioned in Matthew before we get to chapter 17. Our story happens to be the very last one in Matthew, although Luke and John both have Jesus eating fish after the resurrection. I also notice that almost all passages that involve fish in the New Testament are miracle stories.

- I learn by looking at a parallel Gospels book that none of the other Gospels has this particular story in it. That may mean that payment of this tax is of special concern to Matthew and the community for which he wrote his Gospel. That makes sense, because I also have learned that Matthew is particularly interested in showing how Jesus fulfilled the law of the Old Testament.

- I discover from an outline of the Gospel in my study Bible that this story comprises the last three verses of a major section that starts in Matthew 13:54 when Jesus is rejected in Nazareth. *The Access Bible* describes it as a period of "Opposition and acceptance." So I read through this part of the Gospel and note that, indeed, there are many stories there in which Jesus is being challenged by the religious leaders. He is also forming his disciples and accepting the inevitability of his death.

- In terms of form, I notice that there are many other passages in the Gospels, and especially in this section of Matthew, that begin with an official or a disciple asking Jesus a pointed question (see Matthew 15:1; 16:1; 18:1; 18:21; 19:3). In this case, however, the question is asked of Peter and only later clarified by Jesus. This seems to be a new role for Peter and an indication of his status as a recognized leader among the disciples.

3. *The theological content of the text*

What are the theological intentions of the writer? How is God shown to be at work? What images are used for God? Jesus? Human nature? Creation? Salvation? How does the theology of this passage inform, challenge, or provoke you? In my experience, thinking deeply about the theology of the text can be one of the most difficult things for new preachers to grasp. However, it is crucially important to the sermon preparation. After all, you want to be able to describe in your sermon what you think God is up to in this passage, the sort of God that is at work, and the ways that God's people should respond today. Here are some examples, again from Matthew 17:24-27.

- In this passage, Jesus seems to have two supernatural abilities: first, he knows what Peter is going to ask him even before he asks, and second, he predicts the catching of the fish with the coin. Clearly these are miracles that are meant to give the reader more confidence that Jesus is one who knows the minds of others and either knows or controls the future. These claims are part of what theologians call the "Christology" of the Gospel, or in other words, the way the Gospel tries to prove that Jesus is the Christ or Messiah.
- Jesus seems to be concerned less about paying the tax than about not giving offense to people who expect him and his followers to pay the tax. I discover by looking at an Interlinear New Testament in my reading that the verb for giving offense in verse 27 is related to the noun *skandalon*, a word that literally means "stumbling block" and appears soon again in 18:6 and 7, in which Jesus says it's better to be drowned with a millstone than put a *skandalon* in front of others. However, Jesus adds a little saying about the "children of the king" being free from taxation. If Jesus uses the word "king" as a symbol for God, and the king's "children" to mean God's people, then it means that the only reason why they should pay the tax is not because they owe it, but

because if they don't it will scandalize (put a stumbling block in front of) others. This raises many interesting questions about whether followers of Jesus are bound to the Law or free from the Law. Also, what does it mean to think of God as a "king"?

4. The history of the text

Find out as best you can how your text has been used through the ages and is read by people of a different time, culture, denomination, gender, or race than you. Try to see the Bible through the eyes of others. Think, for example, how differently people read the opening chapters of Genesis depending on whether they are evolutionists or new earth creationists. Consider how references to slavery in the New Testament were used to keep slaves in their place in America, and how the Exodus story has been used by African American churches as a source of hope and liberation. How differently do we hear the commandment to keep the Sabbath holy than Jews do, or the Puritans or Scottish Presbyterians did? Think, too, how movies like *The Ten Commandments* or *The Passion of the Christ* have influenced the ways people visualize Bible stories, how Psalm 23 has become a standard reading in funeral services, and 1 Corinthians 13 in weddings, although each was intended for other contexts.

For example, as I read Matthew 17, I wonder how Christians have thought about taxation through the ages and whether there are Christian groups today who have concerns about taxes. I also wonder about how people of different income levels experience the idea of taxes, and how women may respond to the image of God as king, and how professional fishermen in Maine where I live would hear a story about a fish with a coin in its mouth!

There are an increasing number of Bible commentaries and study tools written from the perspectives of different nationalities, ethnicities, genders, sexual identities, and theological perspectives. Reading these will broaden your understanding of scripture and help make your sermons more responsive to the global and diverse world in which we live. For a list of such resources, go to www.pewtopulpit.com.

Explore Your Memories and Images

All of this thinking about the text and the sermon keeps your mind working in the background. New images, memories, stories, quotes, articles, or movies may come into your head to add to those that emerged in your first reading of the text. In my study of Matthew 17, I start to wonder what does it really mean to be free as a child of God? How do I scandalize or offend others? When do I feel offended? What memories or images of stumbling blocks come up for me? I remember that both Luther and Martin Luther King, Jr. had important things to say about Christian freedom. I think about the different religious scandals in the news these days and the effect they have on the church and the world.

At some point I will take time to look these up, often using the Internet. I may dig out an old article on how much people give to churches I once read in *The Atlantic Monthly;* I may remind myself of the film, *Big Fish,* by watching it again or reading about it on the Internet Movie Database (www.imdb.com). I may look up quotes on www.bartleby.com. If I want to pursue the tradition of the fish as an image of Jesus, I might go to a Web site that specializes in images. A simple search turns up the Chinese story I remembered about the man who caught a golden fish. Another yields news articles about the scandals of the day. You get the idea. This part of the sermon preparation is particularly interesting to do.

Turn to the Commentaries

So having now explored this text to the best of your abilities, you can read commentaries by scholars and see how they have read the text. No doubt they will see things that you haven't seen before. Your opinions may change or solidify as you compare your notes to theirs. Whatever happens, now you come more as a peer than as an empty vessel into which you are merely pouring the ideas of others.

This study has likely taken you two or more hours to do. Your notes are becoming so unwieldy that you may want to find a manila folder in which to organize them. You are not yet ready to start writing your sermon, but your mind is bubbling away. You need perspective and a break. Put your work away for a spell again and let it steep a while longer.

CHAPTER 6

Focusing In on Your Message

I t's time to find the forest among the trees of your study. You may be wondering how to find a path through the piles of material you have gathered, or feeling as if you have nothing new to say on a text that has been so picked over by others. Never fear. In this chapter you will wend your way through the thicket and pick up the path of your particular sermon. Along the way you will rediscover your testimony and discover how to preach it with vigor and conviction. Those of you who are intuitive may be way ahead of the process at this point, already certain that you know what your sermon will be about. You will sense rightly that this chapter is an attempt to outline the often inexplicable alchemy that occurs when the preacher opens herself or himself to the movement of the Spirit in the holy company of God's people. Even so, I think it will be useful for you to slow down and consider the following steps to make sure that what you preach is genuinely good news for the congregation and not simply the public display of your inner world. If you are developing a topical sermon rather than a text-based one, you may wish to skip the following section and pick up your reading at "Naming Your Testimony."

"In one of my first sermons I knew exactly what I was going to say, but then I wrote down something completely different for my sermon. The Holy Spirit seemed to be speaking to me, so I let my first idea just float away."

(An Episcopalian training to be a deacon)

Rediscover Your Point of Contact with the Text

Look back at the text again. Read it aloud. Then ask yourself the following questions. You should be able not only to answer each question but also understand and articulate what is going on in your heart or mind that leads you to answer in this way.

- At which level of the text did I connect most deeply? With a specific word or phrase? With a theme touched on by the text, such as justice, sin, the character of God, miracles? With a specific character? With the role of this passage in the flow of the book or its surrounding passages? With the way this passage compares with other similar passages in the Bible? With the intention of the writer or the issue in the community that may have prompted the passage? In other words, if I think of my interest as a camera that is looking over the text, what is it focused upon?
- Now, at what point in the text does it most come alive for me? As I read along is there something that makes my heart leap or troubles me? Something I say "Yes!" to, or disagree with? Where does the passage "hook" me? Why?
- What is the single most exciting and moving thing that I have discovered so far in this process? Do I have a sense that God is speaking to me personally in this passage? Or that I am being challenged in my beliefs, moved emotionally, or provoked to action?

EXAMPLE

How did I connect with Matthew 17:24-27, the fish tale about paying the temple tax? Here are a few of the ways that I feel challenged and moved by this brief passage:

- It is an example of Jesus' perpetual conflict with religious authorities. It made me reflect on who the religious authorities are in the world today with whom Jesus might find himself in conflict. As a theological school professor, I reflect on the troubling question of whether I could bear Jesus' scrutiny of my own use of religious power and authority.

- It is an example of Jesus as a miracle worker. The miracles in this story (reading Peter's mind, predicting a fish with a coin in its mouth) are similar to other Gospel accounts of Jesus having unusual insight into a person or being able to control nature (like stilling the storm). The fish story seems odder than most of the miracle stories I know in the Gospels, however, and I wonder whether such miracles are meant to be taken literally or are still happening today.

- I find that the interaction between Peter and Jesus is a lesson in discipleship. I notice Peter's emerging role as a leader among disciples in Matthew's Gospel, and yet this passage shows how he may still be corrected by the teaching of Jesus. I identify with Peter being stopped short and remember times in my own experiences of leadership when a time of prayer or conversation has changed my approach.

- Jesus' concern about causing scandals or setting out stumbling blocks causes me to meditate on things I say and do that may scandalize others. When I feel the need to speak out on a controversial issue (like where we stand on abortion or war), how do I know for sure whether I am standing up for the gospel, being self-justifying, or creating an unnecessary scandal?

- This text strikes me as a part of the larger question about paying taxes. I find it disturbing that too much of my tax money goes to construct and maintain weapons of mass destruction and too little to help the poor. I wonder if Jesus would consider it more scandalous to pay or not pay taxes today?

- The funny narrative turn about the fish still intrigues me. Why aren't we told that Peter did go and find the fish and the coin? Should we assume it happened or is this just a playful side of Jesus who carefully sidesteps a trap with a strange fish story rather than go along with the tax? Given many of the religious controversies in the news today it makes me wonder whether sometimes those controversies are smokescreens we use to avoid larger issues of faithfulness that confront us.

Look over your original insights and questions and compare them with the study that you have done. Then ask: has my study enlivened, enlarged, or displaced my initial experience of the text? What ongoing questions do I have?

Name Your Testimony

Imagine that you are in a circle of trusted friends, all of whom have been studying the text or discussing the topic of your sermon. Each of you now gets a chance to stand up and share with the group what you have learned about life with God by living with this text or thinking about the topic. There is room for nothing but honesty here, so speak what is really on your heart. If you are preaching from a text and you were able to do the last step, that is, to name how you connected with the text, it is just a small step to boil this down further and state the claim of the text upon you as a person of faith at this time and place. Don't say how this text applies to *others*; say how it applies to you.

If you are developing a topical sermon, be able to state clearly what preaching about this topic means to you personally. What is going on in your heart or mind that has led you to choose this topic out of all the possible ones from which you could choose? What do you intend to do about it personally once the sermon is over? For example, if you decide to preach a sermon on domestic abuse, will you find out about the help resources in your community and connect them in some way? Will you confront an abuser you know or help a victim to find safety? If you preach on the role of prayer, what will you do to deepen your own practice of it?

Whether you begin with a text or a topic, your testimony will involve two things: First, in what way has my study illuminated what God is up to in my life? Second, how is God calling me to respond to this?

EXAMPLE

Here is one testimony I could make about my study of Matthew 17:24-27, the fish tale about paying the temple tax: One of the ways this text caught my attention was that it showed a development of Peter's character as a disciple. It has been my experience in the life of faith that although I am the kind of person who tends to believe things strongly, what I believe has changed through the years. So, I can identify with Peter's experience when he answered the tax collectors one way and then was told privately by Jesus that the life of faith is more complicated than his earlier answer. Over time, this has taught me not to dismiss my strong beliefs, but to be more lighthearted about them and open to the possibility that I may be wrong. Jesus' statement that the "children are free" moves me deeply and contravenes my desire for rules and order. Applied to my own life as a spouse, parent, and teacher, this passage provokes me to remember my place among the free children of grace. God seems more interested in shaping me into a person who loves others as fellow children than in making me a person of unshakeable conviction and unchanging beliefs.

Why Does It Matter to Others?

I must be able to think clearly and with some detachment about the folks who will hear the sermon. Is the testimony that I can give on this text or topic something that is of vital interest to them? How do I know that to be the case? Has it come up as a live issue in the community or is it something I have heard in a conversation? It is quite possible that what intrigues you most about a biblical text is of no vital and practical concern to your community at this time.

The subtle but essential question you have to ask yourself is whether you believe the sermon that is emerging in your mind *is* of vital interest to the congregation, or something that you believe *should be* of vital interest to them. If it is the first, then your hearers will be all ears at the start, although it can be a different story once they hear what you have to say about it. If it is the second, then your sermon will probably meet resistance in the pew: we all resist being told what we ought to do. Sermons are often faced with the task of preaching uphill against the desires of their listeners (after all, who starts out wanting to hear another sermon on stewardship?), so the fact that your sermon should be of vital interest to your congregation (but isn't yet), does not disqualify it from consideration. It does make the task more difficult, however. Wise preachers also will wonder how well they know and accept their congregations if they often find themselves preaching about things their congregation should be interested in but really are not.

The task of this point of sermon development is to be able to articulate as clearly as you did your own testimony of why the developing sermon idea is of vital spiritual importance to the actual congregation who will hear it. Not the imagined congregation of your fantasy preaching life, but the ones who will be facing you from the pew while you are in the pulpit. Your ability in a sermon to quote a French philosopher in the original language or solve a quandary of your family life may satisfy your needs, but probably is not what the church members had on their minds when they woke up earlier and wondered whether it was worth the bother to attend church that day. So think about how your testimony may be heard by the different members of your congregation: the new family from Nigeria that sits in the back, the widowed matriarch whose role in the church is the most important thing left in her life, the eleven-year-old boy whose parent has cancer. As best you can, see your testimony through the eyes of their life experiences.

Write Down a Main Idea

Whether called the focus, theme, thesis statement, topic sentence, or proposition, most teachers of preaching recommend that every sermon have one main idea: the distillation of your testimony to a particular community of people. This should be a single strong sentence: "Because Jesus wrestles with temptation we know that

God understands completely what it means for us to be human." Or, "Just like Jonah the reluctant prophet found out, even a little faith may change the world more than we are comfortable with!" Good main ideas have unity, strength, and interest. They are hopeful proclamations rather than moralistic in tone. They focus more on what God is or has done than on what we should do. Here are some examples of rather weak main ideas drawn from my engagement with Matthew 17, along with stronger alternatives:

- **Weak:** God has given us the freedom of children through Christ.
  Although this is one clear statement and is God-focused, this statement is too brief and inexact to be of much help.
- **Better:** God has made us free in Christ, a freedom that challenges us to grow up in the things we believe.
  This statement is more specific about which dimension of Christian freedom this sermon will discuss.

- **Weak:** Do you know where your taxes go?
  Too brief and vague to guide you in your sermon preparation. Sounds like a political seminar: Where is God in this?
- **Better:** Jesus' cagey answer to the System in his day raises some disturbing questions about what God's will for our finances may be.
  Emphasizes God's action and is more direct and challenging.

- **Weak:** Jesus corrected Peter and taught him to be a better leader and he knows what is on our minds before we say a word.
  There are really two ideas here, one about leadership and one about Jesus' prescience. Neither is well developed. The preacher seems to have two separate sermons in development and needs to make a decision between them.
- **Better:** Jesus' correction of Peter exemplifies the process of becoming a mature disciple: we are introduced into the complexity of the life of faith.
  At first glance this may seem like two ideas, but the words

*after the colon actually add focus to the sermon-to-come
because it clarifies what I mean when I talk about Christian
maturity.*

You get the picture. The main idea is not a clever title for your
sermon, or even a line that has to appear word for word in the
sermon itself. It is a tool to keep you and your sermon focused.

Saying that there should be a main idea in the sermon can
sometimes sound as if that has to come first in its final form
before your sermon writing can go anywhere. It would be nice if
that were always to happen: to figure out exactly what you were
going to say in your sermon and then construct everything from
that point. In real life it is rarely so simple. Many preachers confess to not really knowing what the main idea of the sermon is
until they have conceived half of it. They are struck by an intuition, follow that by a question that haunts them, remember a
parallel story from *Newsweek*, muse over what different scriptures may say about the question, and then come to a decision
about what is really at stake. Sermons that are presented this
way often have the folksy feel of a nice gambol through the
woods, and the clearing may not be apparent until the end of
the journey. But unless they lead to a main point, such sermons
will leave your hearers scratching their heads: what was that sermon about? After all, the point of the sermon is not to intro-
duce us to the intricacies of your thought process, but to
provoke the intricacies of ours. You may arrive at a main idea in
a roundabout fashion, but make sure it is there, something you
can name concretely. It will serve to keep you on track and help
you decide what belongs in your sermon and what should be left
for another.

Write the Purpose Statement

When John the Baptist preached hellfire and damnation, the
crowds came up and begged him to tell them what to do: "Share

your food and clothes," he said. Then the tax collectors and soldiers asked what they should do. "Collect a fair amount," and "don't threaten people," were part of John's response. Similarly, after Peter had preached at Pentecost the crowds were begging Peter and the apostles, "Brothers, what should we do?" They were more than happy to oblige by telling them to repent and be baptized (Acts 2:37-42).

> Some other surprising results of preaching in the New Testament:
> - Getting arrested (John the Baptist, Luke 3:20; Peter and John in Acts 4:3)
> - Enraging a crowd (Acts 7:54)
> - Convincing people to be baptized (Luke 3:21)
> - Putting a child to sleep, who then falls out of a window (Acts 20:9)

Here is what makes preaching different from teaching. Preaching asks for a concrete, bodily response. It is never enough just to offer some thoughts about, say, what a good idea it is to love your neighbor, without at the same time naming what this means to you in real life. Specifically which neighbors? How should I love them? What would be the risks and consequences of such love? Jesus was asked precisely that question by an impatient listener, so he told the story of the good Samaritan. In a word, love the one you most abhor.

So, now that you have a main idea for your sermon, the question is: "So what?" What is your sermon trying to achieve? In what way will the world be different because you preached this sermon? What would you have us do, think, or be differently? And what is more, how will this sermon move us to do it?

Sermons can do many more things than we may realize. They can move, excite, inspire, provoke, or comfort us. They can lead us to question, encourage or discourage our actions, cause us to daydream, waste our time, or bore us to tears. But no sermon goes by without something happening for good or ill in the lives of the hearers.

CENTER OF GRAVITY

I classify sermons as three types according to their "center of gravity": head, heart, or gut. That is, they can set out to change the mind, affect the heart, or move the body. I have come to believe that we would do well to lower the center of gravity of much of our preaching, aiming at the heart and gut more often than the head. Growing, lively churches are usually those whose preaching stimulates us to feel and act on, not just think about, the life of faith. But not all preaching traditions would agree: Presbyterian and Congregationalist preaching, for example, historically prides itself on its intellectualism. Here are some examples of the purposes a sermon may have depending upon its center of gravity.

Head sermons are those that expect:
• To convince us of a new way of understanding something
• To persuade us that something is true or false
• To teach a point about something, like a doctrine, an interpretation of the Bible, or the meaning of the liturgical season
• To inform us about a social issue or concern
• To notify about plans or projects in the congregation
• To open our eyes to an insight about God or life

Heart sermons are those that desire:
• To create a sense of sorrow for sin or the joy of forgiveness
• To help us feel the presence of God in a new way
• To stir our hearts to the plight of the poor
• To inspire us to dream
• To reassure us of God's love
• To evoke our awe and praise at something God has done

Gut sermons are those that try:
• To generate spiritual growth
• To lead us to a place of calmness or meditation
• To enlist us for a mission trip
• To call people to leadership in the church
• To energize our devotion to God or a religious cause
• To inspire us to give more money or build a new building

A sermon may do more than one thing and some persons who hear it may be prompted to think while others are moved to act. Nevertheless, to be clear what your primary purpose is, the next step is to write a *purpose statement*. Like your main idea, a purpose statement should be a strong single sentence. It should begin with an infinitive (the word "To" and a strong action verb). The purpose statement sums up why you are preaching the sermon. What are you trying to achieve? How will the congregation or world be different after you preached?

> The old Puritan preachers, William Ames and Charles Chauncey, used to emphasize that a sermon could have five different applications or purposes. The first four were based on 2 Timothy 3:16-17, and the last on 1 Corinthians 14:3:
> * To inform of a truth
> * To refute an error
> * To correct wrong behaviors
> * To exhort good behaviors and inward virtues
> * To comfort people in grief or fear

Here are some examples of rather weak purpose statements followed by some that are more useful.

Weak: To help us consider that we should trust God when things get hard.
The extra verbs "help" and "consider" are indirect and almost apologetic in tone. To consider something is clearly a head-centered approach, whereas trusting is for most folks more a heart or gut-centered response.
Stronger: To move us to rely on God.
This is more direct. This sermon will have a lower center of gravity.

Weak: To encourage us to think about how we are connected with others across the world.
Again, a head sermon that uses vague words. It is a huge topic and frankly rather an insipid response for a sermon.

Stronger: To raise enthusiasm and money for the mission trip to Costa Rica.

If this is the need in the congregation, don't hesitate to name it directly. As hearers we will know anyway what your real purpose is, so don't beat around the bush!

Weak: To challenge us to have a deeper desire for a relationship with God.

The idea of challenge is action or gut-centered while desire is heart-centered. The theology is weak, too, for God is already in relationship with us, whether we know it or not.

Better: To evoke a deep desire to respond to God's call for us to pray more often.

Feelings are evoked, not challenged into existence. The purpose is a far more specific here.

Weak: To teach about the injustices in our present tax system.
A fine head-centered sermon appropriate for a political rally.

Better: To teach what the Bible and United Methodist traditions have to say about justice and taxpaying.

This sermon will teach us about a current issue from the perspective of our Christian faith and church traditions.

Note that the stronger the purpose the more honest your sermon will be. Fuzzy purpose statements often reflect a preacher's anxiety or uncertainty about the reason for a particular message. A caution is also in order. In my experience, a preponderance of sermons by newer preachers tend to have "to reassure" as their purpose. There are times when being reassured is exactly the right message for any congregation. But a constant diet of it takes the edge off the life of faith, and, frankly, doesn't do justice to the wide varieties of proclamations that appear in scripture.

The Main Metaphor

In his book, *Preaching Without Notes*, Joseph Webb helpfully suggests that every sermon should have a "controlling metaphor" closely related to the main idea. Scripture is full of marvelous

A purpose statement should be related to the main idea of your sermon. A sermon whose main idea is the topic of hospitality to strangers, for example, would founder if its purpose were, "To move people to conversion," rather than something like: "To teach Jewish traditions about welcoming strangers," or "To challenge people to support the city's homeless ministry." Here are two examples of sermons that I have preached that show how I have tried to match the purpose statement with the main idea.

FOR A SERMON ABOUT THE CHRISTIAN COMMUNITY IN ACTS 2

- Main Idea: Here are the deep secrets of Christian community: Sticking it out together; refusing to leave; and sharing the condition of the flock.
- Purpose: To move the congregation to spend more time together in fellowship and worship (gut-centered).

FOR A SERMON ON THE PRODIGAL SON

- Main Idea: God's grace extends to both our responsible and irresponsible selves.
- Purpose: To evoke our experience of God's correcting love, helping us to live by grace, not by over-responsibility (heart-centered).

metaphors: God is like a potter (Jeremiah); coming judgment is like a plumb line (Amos); Jesus is like a hen gathering chicks (Matthew and Luke). These are strong, rich, and memorable metaphors that can be explored deeply by the imagination and reveal many important insights into the secret of faithful living. It is not too much to say that a vital metaphor can act as an organizing principle for the Christian life. So, in addition to a main idea and purpose statement, you may find that your sermon will achieve unity if you use a central metaphor to guide you. The more playful the better. I often find that the central metaphor ends up being a good sermon title. Here are a couple of examples from recent sermons I have preached.

For a sermon about spiritual friends: Friends are those who help you when you are at the end of your rope (at the end we handed out small bits of rope to the congregation to keep in their pockets).

For the sermon about the temple tax and the coin in the fish's mouth: Fishing for Change.

Patterns and Forms

You have a main idea and a purpose statement for your sermon. Along the way you have generated a lot of other material as well: personal anecdotes, news stories, similar Bible passages, and so on. Now, how do you assemble those ideas into a coherent event? How do you arrange your sermon material so that people won't just understand the gospel, but actually experience it? This is the question of sermon form, or simply how you purposefully arrange your material to make your message clear and maximize the impact.

We use forms all the time in oral speech: the knock-knock joke, or the casual greeting: "How are you?" "Fine, how are you?" Jesus employed forms regularly: the reversal ("you have heard it said, but I say to you"), the proclamation ("truly, truly I tell you"), the beatitude ("blessed are those who"), and most famously, the parable ("the kingdom of heaven is like").

Many experienced preachers never give a thought to sermon form. The better ones either know intuitively how to arrange their material or adopt a couple of forms unconsciously. Have you ever listened to a preacher several weeks in a row and discovered that she or he typically has three points in a sermon, or always starts with a personal story? If so, then you have stumbled onto part of that preacher's regular form. In your own preaching, it is better for you adopt forms consciously than to fall into ruts unknowingly. Further, if you can think ahead about the forms you use you will find that composing the sermon will be much easier. Not only that, your hearers will be grateful because a good form lends energy or forward movement to a sermon and helps us follow along.

There are many possible patterns that you may choose: some preachers preach verse by verse, commenting on each passage along the way; others like to retell the story from a fresh perspective, filling in details from one of the characters perhaps; still others begin with a question and then use their sermon to spin out an answer. In this chapter we will learn a few simple forms with which you are probably already familiar.

Deduce or Induce?

A *deductive sermon* starts with the main idea and then unfolds it or explains it as the sermon continues. It may look something like this:

1. An introduction, such as an anecdote or story that touches on the main idea.
2. The main idea.
3. Two or three points that illustrate, prove, or expand upon the main idea. This is the main body of your sermon.
4. An application about what it means for faithful living.
5. A conclusion, perhaps recalling or finishing the introduction.

The benefit of deductive patterns is that they are clear and logical. If done well there should be no confusion in the hearer about the main point of the sermon because it is stated right up front. A potential problem in this pattern is that because the punch line is given away at the beginning, there may be little suspense or interest for some listeners. Yet there is still plenty of room for creativity here depending on how engaging your introduction and subpoints may be. Listeners who like to take notes and have unambiguous marching orders will bless you for this style.

An *inductive sermon* is one in which the main idea may not become clear until the end, or near the end of the sermon. It may look like this:

1. An introduction that leads to a question or problem (Did you notice that this story never mentions that Peter actually found a fish with a coin? or, Have you ever thought what it would mean for your faith if we discovered life on another planet?).
2. The relevance of the issue for our own lives is explored, perhaps through a series of illustrations and anecdotes. Different sides of a debate may be explored.
3. The biblical text is revisited in such a way that the question is highlighted.
4. A clue for resolution is discovered.
5. The main idea is put forth.
6. A conclusion invites the listeners to live more deeply into the question than they had previously.

The benefit of the inductive sermon is that when done well it creates suspense and interest. Listeners will be intrigued by the problem stated in the introduction and lean forward in their seats until the main idea becomes clear. Advocates of this pattern say that such structures are more listener-friendly because they mimic the way human beings tell stories and that they feel more conversational than preachy. Further, they exemplify the journey of faithful reflection, sharing the process of discovery that the preacher underwent in preparing the sermon. If done well, the listener should have the same "aha" experience that the preacher experienced when she or he was exploring the text or topic. However, if the sermon in fact does not build suspense, then there will be no "aha" at the end and your hearers may wonder what the sermon was about. Such sermons may also be less satisfying to those who like to take notes.

Follow the Pattern of the Biblical Text

Another option is to let the pattern of the biblical text shape the pattern of your sermon. For example, a sermon on Psalm 42 could follow the terrain of the emotions experienced in the psalm itself.

1. The experience of God's absence (vv. 1-3)
2. Memories of a time when God felt present (4)
3. Trying to have faith in exile and suffering (5-7, 9-10)
4. Prayer for God's remembrance (7-8)
5. Affirmation of hope (11)

One of the three temptations of Jesus in Matthew 4:1-11:

1. The harshness of the desert (1-2)
2. The temptation to use God (3-4)
3. The temptation to test God (5-7)
4. The temptation of idolatry (8-10)
5. Triumph over evil (11)

Conflict-Pattern-Resolution

If you have ever watched a classic situation comedy like *Leave It to Beaver, Gilligan's Island,* or *Frasier,* then you have been initiated into one of the most compact formulas for telling a story: conflict, pattern, resolution. Gilligan meets a stranded cosmonaut who will have room for only two people on the rescue ship, two by two the castaways bribe the cosmonaut with coconut juice until he gets sick, so sick that a hilarious chase scene ensues, after which the cosmonaut leaves, Gilligan is forgiven, and the castaways reaffirm their acceptance of one another. I'll grant you that most of these shows are mindless drivel, but rather than despairing over how American culture is going down the tubes, we should ask why these shows enjoy such enormous popularity. For one thing, at twenty-two minutes (not counting the commercials), they are concise. They move forward with no distracting fat. And, they stick closely to the formula of conflict, pattern, and resolution.

In his classic book, *The Homiletical Plot*, Eugene Lowery has elaborated this form for preaching as "Oops, Ugh, Aha! Whee! Yeah."

Oops: a problem or question is noted.

Ugh: the seriousness of the problem is developed.

Aha!: the clue for the resolution is hinted at.

Whee!: The resolution is experienced as relief and exhilaration

Yeah: The meaning of this for our lives is made clear.

THE UGLY DUCKLING

- Oops: Large ugly duckling hatched; Duckling continually rejected by the ducks.
- Ugh: The Ugly Duckling sees the most beautiful of all birds: white swans. Winter passes; spring comes.
- Aha!: Two children point at the ugly duckling and say, "Look! A new swan! He's even more beautiful than the others." At first he thinks they are making fun.
- Whee!: He looks at his own reflection.
- Yeah: The other swans call out to him in welcome.

NOAH

This form is common in the biblical world. Consider the story of Noah from Genesis 6:11–9:17):
- Oops: The world is full of sin.
- Ugh: A flood is on its way.
- Aha!: Noah builds an ark.
- Whee!: The ark survives.
- Yeah: God establishes a new covenant.

Pattern, Breaking of Pattern, Resolution

Another common way of organizing a story is to establish a pattern of expectation, build up the intensity, and then suddenly reverse it. Think of children's stories such as the Three Little Pigs, Little Red Riding Hood, or the Three Billy Goats Gruff: Three characters want something (sweet green grass on the other side). They meet an obstacle (the troll); the first two characters set a pattern and build anticipation ("my brother is coming after me, and he's much fatter than me"); then comes a surprise reversal (big Billy Goat Gruff knocks the troll off the bridge); and the resolution (they eat the grass together in peace). This form often appears in scripture, especially in parables such as the Parable of the Sower (Matthew 13:2-9), the Laborers in the Vineyard (Matthew 20:1-16), and the Talents (Matthew 25:14-30).

Compare and Contrast

One easy form is the simple contrast or comparison, the either/or or the both/and. Jesus contrasted those who build their houses on sand with those that build on rock; he compared the wise and foolish bridesmaids, and the sheep and the goats. He also used both/and: new wine is put into fresh wineskins (Matthew 9:17); fear those who can destroy both the body and soul (Matthew 10:28); both debtors are forgiven (Luke 7:42).

The Four Pages of the Sermon

Paul Scott Wilson teaches his students a very effective form built on a central analogy or comparison between what happened in the Bible and what is happening in our world today.
- Trouble in the Bible: a problem or condition of sin is noted in the text.

- Trouble in the World: this reveals a parallel problem or condition in the world today.
- Grace in the Bible: the operation of God's grace is seen in the midst of the trouble.
- Grace in the World: God's grace is seen operating in the world today.

He emphasizes that these pages may be reshuffled, so the preacher may choose to start with Trouble in the World, or move from Trouble in the Bible to Grace in the Bible. Besides its simplicity, a great benefit here is the clear God-centeredness of such sermons. Less interested in what we should do, they emphasize what God is already doing. While this style is very useful and popular among new preachers, a necessary caution is for the preacher to be aware that not every text is applicable to every congregation, and that some analogies actually diminish the power of scripture. For example, is contemporary spiritual captivity really similar to Israel's slavery under Egypt? Can a fair analogy be drawn between the martyrdom of Stephen and some Christians today being dismayed that public praying in the name of Jesus is not allowed by school officials?

I hope you understand by now that the form you choose is more than a scaffold on which you build your sermon. Your form influences not only how you say something, but indeed, what you say. It may help to think of your sermon as a work of art and the form as the medium. How differently would we experience Michelangelo's David had he sculpted it in bronze rather than marble? Or if the Rolling Stones had made "Satisfaction" a folk song rather than rock and roll? How differently will we experience your sermon if you tell it like a story, argue it like a case, offer it like a question, or raise it as a hope?

CHAPTER 8

Crafting Your Message

Write in the Language of the Ear

Unlike when we are reading, when we are listening to a sermon we cannot go back and reread a sentence until we get it. The words pass us by and then move on. Therefore good oral speech is direct and simple. It avoids jargon and complex constructions. It uses active (Jesus raised Lazarus) rather than passive voice (Lazarus was raised by Jesus). It is not afraid of using repetition. It thrives on short words and vivid verbs. It flounders on unnecessarily complex and unhelpfully convoluted academic-sounding verbiage and long sentences that run on and on like this one. It really dies agonizingly on adverbs.

If you are preparing to preach without notes, picture the sermon in your head as a series of scenes that flow together like a film, or a series of pages from a children's book that lead one to another. If you doubt that you can preach a sermon without notes, ask yourself whether you are able to tell the story of Goldilocks to a young child without reading from a book. Most of us can. If you can't remember your sermon like this, chances are that it is too complicated. Could our sermons be so intriguing and inviting that we could have our listeners on the edge of their seats, asking themselves eagerly, "Yes, and what comes next?" instead of "Hmm, I wonder where this is this going?" or, "Is it nearly time for coffee?"

Talk Out Your Sermon Aloud as You Write

However I deliver them, I still write most of my sermons. But I do so with a closed door because I write loudly. I speak the sermon, typing as I go. This way, the words stay smaller and the constructions simpler. I also find that there are word combinations that please the tongue while others just taste thick and unappealing. I'll often notice when the sermon seems stuck, it is because I've stopped speaking aloud and am staring at the screen. Then I back up, often to the very beginning, and make another run at it. Usually this breaks the logjam. Sometimes the mouth knows how the sermon needs to proceed in a way that fingers and the brain alone cannot.

Make It Come Alive

Create Interest at the Start. When in doubt about where to start your sermon, try beginning with the central conflict or the most emotional illustration or story. This lets us know that what follows is important and worth listening to. It often also cuts out unnecessary preamble.

Use Repetition. Don't be afraid of it. Use repetition. How much of Martin Luther King's sermon would we remember if he hadn't framed paragraph after paragraph with: "I have a dream?" So, use repetition.

The "Call Back." An old trick of the stand-up comedy trade is to finish a set with a reference to a joke told earlier. This is an effective way to work out your conclusion.

The most skillful sermons break rules of grammar, leave things out, and repeat themselves—just like real human conversations do.

The unfinished sentence left hanging. Let people fill in. Jesse Jackson's "I am Somebody" became so famous that the crowds would fill in the last word. "I am," he would say, and the crowd yelled, "SOMEBODY!"

Avoid stilted words and tired phrases: "Indeed!" and "As we approach the throne of grace."

Cut out the fat: be ruthless about cutting out portions of your sermon that do not actively contribute to the main idea and purpose. This is one of the hardest things to do in preaching. It is not uncommon for me to discover that the lovely and stirring

Richard Dowis, the author of *The Lost Art of the Great Speech,* emphasizes that any good speech uses active verbs and vivid nouns, what he calls "gut words." It is concrete not abstract. He gives as an example a selection from Winston Churchill's "Finest Hour Speech." This was a radio address to the nation of Britain in September 1940, after the fall of France to the Nazis, a desperate time when Britain felt alone and besieged.

> We shall not flag or fail. We shall go on to the end. We shall fight in France. We shall fight on the seas and oceans. We shall fight with growing confidence and growing strength in the air. We shall defend our island, whatever the cost may be. We shall fight on the beaches. We shall fight on the landing grounds. We shall fight in the fields and in the streets. We shall fight in the hills. We shall never surrender.

There are eighty-one words here. Of these, only eleven have more than one syllable, and of these nine words, only three have more than two. Also note the repetition. Each of the short sentences begins with the two words, "We shall . . . " The cumulative effect is that the words build energy. Matched by Churchill's teeth-clenched voice, this speech created within the hearts of a fearful nation exactly the kind of fighting determination it described. The words didn't just describe what the Brits ought to do: they made it happen.

passage I have just written really doesn't belong in this particular sermon, but needs to be saved for a later date (or tossed). I liken preaching to the process of boiling ten gallons of maple sap to make one gallon of syrup.

Finally, be concrete! Beginning preachers more often feel the need to say too much than too little. Sermons that, for example, try to make a statement about the current state of the world often fall into the trap of listing as many horrible things as they can think of (war, sexism, racism, violence, unemployment, drug abuse, and so on) without dealing with any one of them in particular. But the power is in the personal; it is in the story. If you want us to be moved to respond to them with gospel fervor, don't tell us about them, give us a single story. Show us the one child living in poverty whose life was turned around by Christian caring. The network news departments have learned this lesson well: it is more powerful to portray the story of a single man who lost his family in a drunk-driving accident than just to give statistics.

The Voice of Your Sermon

Should your sermon be predominantly in first person "I" and "we and us"; second person, "you"; or third person, "he, she, it, and them"? Good preaching uses all of these voices for particular reasons.

Telling stories in the first person singular (I), or talking about "my reading of this text," or "my experience" is unavoidable when you understand preaching as testimony. The great gift of this voice is that you take a stand in your particularity, inviting others to overhear. One hazard is egoism: nothing is more embarrassing than hearing preachers tell stories in which they are always the hero or the goat. First person plural ("we/us") language can create a sense of community in the sermon, but it can also exclude. When you are inclined to use "we" language, ask yourself, who is "we"? Who is not included in that "we"?

Second person ("you") language, is very direct. It can be experienced either as pastoral or paternalistic. Good caregivers use "you" language a lot because they attend closely to the experience of others. On the other hand, preachers who use "you" in such a way that it places them above their congregations generate understandable negative reactions.

Third person plural ("they") language, can help ensure the recognition of appropriate otherness and authenticity of people who have different experiences from us. But third person plural can easily degenerate into "us versus them," which is religious poison.

Sermonic Mood

A sermon has an emotional landscape. This will vary widely with the purpose of your sermon, whether it is aimed at the head, heart, or gut, of course, but even a head-centered sermon doesn't have to be emotionally colorless. Effective sermons usually reach their emotional peak just before their conclusions, just as TV sitcoms do.

Perhaps you can think of it as the fluctuation of intensity. Is it predominantly casual? Earnest? Humorous? Lighthearted? Sad? Heavy? Be sure to vary the tone of your preaching within a sermon, and from sermon to sermon. Beware especially of being overly earnest, a common trap of the new preacher.

Preaching in a Visual Age

Preaching was birthed from an oral culture but now swims in an electronic and visual one: film, television, Web sites, graphic novels, and simplified newspapers with bar charts in the corner. Our brains process visual information very quickly, images rush past us leaving impressions and creating moods. A television commercial fluttering images of young people dancing and flirting at different parties sets a mood of high energy and urgent desire, long before the product itself is revealed: an ordinary beer.

Preaching is a doubtful and outdated technology for reaching masses of people with a message. If you were to stand on the street corner and preach today you would be ignored by most, thought a lunatic by some, and given spare change by the rest. However, self-selected groups of people will still tune in or lean in to hear a lone person with a microphone who can make them laugh, tell them how to invest their money, or give them advice about the ten ways not to mess up their lives. For me, this means that no matter how wired we become, people still respond to a person with convictions who stands up to tell it like it is.

USING VISUAL MEDIA WITH YOUR SERMON: PRO AND CON

Pro:
- We live in a visual age. As Paul said, "I will be all things to all people."
- We process visual media more quickly than language
- More and more churches are doing it, creating an expectation that it should be done
- It is helpful for the hearing-impaired
- It especially appeals to the younger generations
- Great resources are now available to help us do it well

Con:
- Electronic media and equipment can be expensive
- Many of our churches' worship spaces are not set up for it
- We have never done it that way (the famous last words of many churches)
- I don't have time to add an extra step to my preparation
- It's called idolatry, folks. Worshiping the image . . .
- Electronic things break down
- It is just one more concession to American consumerist entertainment culture—the gospel should free us from that
- Multimedia sermons try to control too many senses. Good preaching should free up the imaginations of the hearers, not funnel them all in a predetermined way.

Many churches are discovering that worship services and sermons that feature amplified music and projected images (such as film clips, photos, art, or Bible passages) better suit the expectations of their media savvy congregations and can move them more deeply. Those that do it well invest in good equipment and take time to train people how to use it. They also develop a worship team and plan preaching ahead, knowing that these extra steps require teamwork. My students and I experiment regularly with the use of visual media in preaching, knowing that well-chosen images can supplement powerful words, but that bad preaching with good images is still simply bad preaching.

C H A P T E R 9

Final Preparations

The Paper It's Printed On

*"Twice I have opened my folder at the pulpit expecting to
pull out my sermon (I preach mostly from a manuscript)
only to discover I did not have it!! Ironically, my 'off the
cuff' sermons are met with more enthusiasm than some of
what I consider to be my better-written ones!"*
(A United Methodist Local Lay Pastor)

We sometimes mistakenly call the words that we put on
a page or type into our computers as "my sermon," as
in the question: "Would you like to have a copy of my
sermon?" What the local pastor discovered when she opened her
folder was that her sermon was not what was contained on the
page, but what was in her heart. It was the collection of sounds
uttered by her mouth and processed by the brains of the congregation, not what was printed on a page. Sermons that rely on
manuscripts and those that use no notes at all are alike in that
both are oral, spoken events.

Nevertheless, preachers carry paper of all sorts into the pulpit on Sunday morning: a fistful of index cards, notes folded in a jacket-pocket, a plain manila folder neatly holding bleached white 20-bond paper, a big floppy Bible with preaching notes scribbled in the margins. Whatever you choose to use, find something that does not call attention to itself. No need to hide your papers as if they didn't exist. The congregation can't be fooled. But don't wave them about either. How often have you witnessed this scene? A speaker walks up to a podium, takes a sandwich of paper out of a breast pocket, holds it in front of the microphone while unfolding it noisily, flattens it out, clears his or her throat, looks down, and then starts to read. Everything about that little ritual communicates that the speaker is dead nervous and that the speech that follows will be dry and formal. Better to take your printed pages and place them in the pulpit before the worship service begins.

If you plan to use a manuscript, take advantage of computer technology and print it out in large type (at least 14 points), and double-space your lines, so that you can see it clearly and easily from a standing posture. Most manuscript preachers today write their sermons on the computer and use standard 8½-x-11-inch paper, because this is what the printer's paper tray holds. Others find that a smaller half-page works better with the size of the pulpit desk. A few I know, often those who find writing by computer cramps their creativity, write out longhand on yellow legal paper. Whatever size paper you use, keep your page margins wide, about one and one-half inches all around. This allows you to grasp the page without your thumbs getting in the way, and gives you room to make additions or revisions at the time of final review.

Preach through the sermon without stopping at least once or twice to get a sense of how long it will be. Read the sermon to another person (a willing spouse?) who will be candid enough to tell you if he or she can follow the train of thought in your sermon.

Once you know your sermon very well, it may feel more comfortable for you to turn the manuscript into a one or two-page set of notes, taking that into the pulpit instead. Others write the whole manuscript out because they think best by writing or they just wish to get the flow of the words right. Then they learn it by heart and go into the pulpit with no notes at all.

If you use a manuscript when you preach, prepare it well so you don't come across like you are reading it to the congregation.

Print it out in big (at least 14 point) type,

Use 1-1/2 lines of spacing between lines.

Line it out phrase by phrase,

like breathing,

the way we really speak.

Not all run together like written prose.

Use large margins on left and right.

Remember to number the pages.

Go through your manuscript with a pen,

<u>underline</u> emphasized words.

Write a vertical mark where you want to pause. Memorize at least the opening few sentences, and the closing sentences, and practice the whole sermon enough times that you will find you have much of it dancing on the tip of your tongue, even if you don't plan to memorize the whole thing.

The Preaching Space

Here is something that I wish someone had said to me early on: you have permission to make the preaching space work for you. I once preached as a guest at a church where the red velvet preacher's chair was barely six inches away from the back of the pulpit. Compounding matters was the fact that the pulpit was near the back of a very long room, unnaturally far from the congregation. I arrived late and didn't want to make a fuss. The pastor showed me to the seat behind the pulpit and then walked back to take a seat on the pews, leaving me alone in the chancel area. When I sat, I couldn't see a thing, and when I stood to sing or to preach I felt like my legs were being held prisoner. Had I been bolder (or arrived earlier) I would have requested that the chair be moved, or a portable lectern or even a music stand be brought in that was closer to the congregation. My sermon was as constrained that morning as my body felt.

If you are new to preaching you may not be familiar with what pulpits look like from behind—answer: not nearly as nice as they look from the pews. They are often cluttered with out-of-date hymnals, matches, old candles, and dubious cups of water. The straight-backed chairs can be appallingly uncomfortable. The preaching desk itself (the flat place on top) may contain an old Bible (never used anymore, but given by Uncle Cyrus and so untouchable), pencils, ancient sermon notes, and the upper portion of the pulpit parament, all held in place by the Bible, so if you move the Bible the whole arrangement comes crashing down. Clearly you will feel less free to rearrange the furniture wholesale in a church in which you are an interim or guest preacher. But even so, don't be overly shy. Get something to stand on if the pulpit is too high (some preachers of small stature carry a wooden box with them), and clear the space as you need. Get there early enough to get the feel for the space before the service begins, adjust the pulpit if it can be adjusted, and become comfortable with the view. Scan the room and note the different seating sections: how far back are the last pews, usually the most popular seats in the house? Is there anything that hides my view of the side aisles? Where will the choir sit? Note in advance how you will have to turn your body to include people with your eyes.

If you are preaching with notes or a manuscript, put those in the pulpit before the worship service begins so that you don't have to carry them up or pull them out of your pocket like a magician's handkerchief. Putting them out of reach in the pulpit can also help you resist any urge to study them during the opening hymn.

"Amen!" wrote one student in response to this point: "If you don't know the sermon by now you aren't going to learn it in five minutes!"

Microphones

Today, sound systems are usually integrated into new church construction. Larger congregations may have elaborate systems for speech and music, and sound "techies" to operate them. But traditional and smaller churches may resist sound systems. Some of this resistance comes from their love of the natural sound of the human voice, and some from their experiences of very poor systems in other churches. Many of these systems were installed by well-meaning congregation members who wanted to save some dollars by picking up a few things at the local electronics store. If your congregation is thinking about adding a sound system, flee like the devil from the temptation to do-it-yourself. Getting a system that makes the spoken word more intelligible will likely require help by a professional, and significant financial outlay, but the reward is incredible clarity.

The English language relies to an unusual degree on high-frequency sounds such as "t" and "s" and the long "e." But it is precisely the higher frequencies that are hardest to hear by people whose hearing is poor or declining. Even smaller churches these days are installing microphone and sound systems, not because the overall volume of the human voice is insufficient to fill the room anymore, but as an act of loving regard for its hearing-impaired members. Hearing assist devices, microphones, and well-placed speakers can work wonders for congregational comprehension and participation in the service. So, if offered use of a microphone, don't automatically refuse it even if you think your voice is large enough to carry to the back pew. It may also be hooked up to a cassette recorder making tapes for shut-ins.

You will encounter all kinds of microphones if you preach for a while: gooseneck, lapel, omnidirectional, boundary, and so on. The good news is that microphone technology has advanced and the newer ones are more forgiving. But here are a number of things to remember.

- Adjust it so that it points to your mouth.
- Turn it on before you preach.
- Keep spare batteries for lapel mics.
- Turn it off afterwards, especially if you use a lapel mic. The urban legend of the pastor who left the microphone on while going to the bathroom is reason enough to be careful. There is a story around here of a pastor who whispered, "another one bites the dust" as the bride and groom were walking down the aisle.
- If the microphone is fixed, don't lean in to it, but don't lean back either. Moving toward and away from a microphone can cause large variations in volume.
- Preach to the congregation and not at the mic. Speak naturally and strongly. One common tendency of newer preachers is to reduce the volume of their speaking voice when they know they are in a presence of a microphone or hear themselves over the sound system. But this reduces the range of vocalizations they can use and makes the sermon feel emotionally flatter. So preach as you normally would and let the sound system enhance, not reduce, your vocal range and volume. Skilled preachers may even experiment with using a mic to "whisper secrets" to the congregation, and draw them in.

A final word: it bears saying that a vital part of preparing to preach is to get plenty of rest and exercise. Pure adrenaline will get you through one sermon but is not a plan for a lifetime of preaching.

CHAPTER 10

Giving Your Sermon

Spoken, Not Written

Christian preaching is about speaking, not about writing. The Christian movement was a movement of the spoken Word long before it had letters and Gospels to read to one another. Because preaching is a spoken Word, it is an event, an occasion in time. This changes everything. As an art, preaching then is very much more like music or theatre than it is like other forms of short writing, such as essays and stories. A sermon is a pattern of sound waves that move through the air. It happens, and then it's over. What matters is less what the preacher intended to say than what was actually heard by the congregation, what together the preacher and hearers create in the time set aside for preaching and in the way they live their lives afterward.

Words are only a small part of that creativity. And unlike putting words on a printed page, only a small portion of that event is under the control of a preacher. So many strange things can happen when a group of living, breathing, human beings get together in a room. Besides babies crying, cell phones ringing, and trains rattling by, people walk in late or walk out early.

Remarkably, congregations usually agree pretty much when to sit, when to stand, when to speak, and when to listen. But sometimes people don't go along with what the crowd says: they'll stand up and argue with you, or raise a hand and ask a question and make your carefully prepared sermon go off in a different direction. They will frown, grunt, laugh, applaud, pass gas, and generally do the things that human bodies do.

So never consider the sermon a set performance piece that you have to get through that morning, come hell or high water. Remaining flexible will be very hard to do if you have prepared a thoughtful manuscript into which you have poured your passion and your prayers. But there will be a time when you hear on your way from the parking lot into the church that a beloved member of your community has just died, or a hurricane has taken out the town where the previous pastor is now living and she needs your congregation's help. These are the times when you may decide to set aside your prepared sermon (or the whole service) and lead the congregation in prayer and conversation about what is really on their hearts that morning.

The Last Shall Be First

"I thought you seemed at ease."

"Good voice. I could hear everything you said, and it seemed natural."

"When you reached out your hand to us at the very end, it got me right here!"

These kinds of observations are invariably the very first things to be said in sermon feedback sessions in which I have been a part. It is amazing to me: no matter how carefully listeners are prepared to listen for the main idea, the use of scripture, the ways illustrations are used, or the form of the sermon, a sermon's performance is the first thing they want to talk about. For years I fought this as a teacher. I would tell a class specifically that we wouldn't hear any comments on sermon delivery until we considered everything else first. But after a while, I quit fighting this human reality and decided to learn from it. I noticed that even if the feedback started with the delivery, it never simply got stuck there. The conversation flowed organically into reflection on all the important aspects of the sermon. In the end, I found most listeners seem to judge a sermon as effective or ineffective based on what they had heard the preacher actually say and whether it moved them religiously. But like the power of a first impression, the delivery either opened their ears or closed them down.

Ronald Allen, who teaches preaching at Christian Theological Seminary in Indianapolis, has suggested that it would be better to use the word "embodiment" rather than delivery. I agree. Deliveries are what postal workers do: they deposit hand packets of paper, prepared by someone else, into empty boxes. But as we have seen, a congregation is anything but a collection of empty boxes and a sermon event is quite different from a pre-prepared, pre-wrapped package. You embody your sermon in a web of relationships, in a room of active, engaged human bodies thinking and feeling about all kinds of things all at once. The timbre of your voice, the sparkle in your eyes, the boldness of your gesture, the clothes you wear, the personality you project, and all the other tangible things you are bring the sermon to life. These are generally the last things we think about as we prepare our sermons, but they seem to be the first things people experience. I'm a balding, middle-aged, white Euro-American man, whose accent has been shaped by years living in the South, and whose body shape reveals me to be neither an athlete nor entirely a couch potato. When I am nervous—and I still get nervous when I preach—like many other people, I speak too fast and too softly. I drop the ends of my sentences and fail to make eye contact. For good or ill, this is the "clay jar" (2 Corinthians 4:7) in which my sermons are embodied. Being honestly aware of your body, how it feels, how it looks, and how others perceive it is fundamental to good preaching embodiment. How can you be honest about the gospel if you are not honest about yourself?

Speaking of Nerves

A student was scheduled to preach for the second time in my seminary preaching class. She had done excellent work during the semester, and had preached a fine first sermon only a few weeks before. But she was still not used to being in the pulpit, and today she looked unusually anxious. She had chosen to preach a sermon that was on the cutting edge of her life with God. She wasn't sure how it would be received or even whether she would be able to get through some of it, her emotions were so high. As the class was still getting settled, I quietly checked in with her. "Are you OK?" I asked. "No," she replied sharply, "is that a prerequisite to preaching?"

Surveys of people's worst fears reveal that public speaking is one of the things we most dread, even more than death. Add to that the sacred dimension of speaking in a church setting (or even worse, a seminary classroom!) and preaching can feel insurmountable. But in my experience, some of the very best preachers are the ones that are most anxious about it. They are thoughtful people who craft passionate sermons in the study—full of wit, conviction, and careful observations about God and the world. If you ask them, though, they might tell you that they would rather hand over the sermon for someone else to deliver. The very thought terrifies them. It is a measure of God's sense of humor that so many people who are called to preach are quiet persons, without the booming voices or big personalities you might think are needed for filling a sanctuary. Paul himself noted that he sometimes came across more powerfully in his writing than in person. His critics in Corinth would say with disdain: "His letters are weighty and strong, but his bodily presence is weak, and his speech contemptible" (2 Corinthians 10:10).

On the other hand, introspection is a gift that can help us guard against saying foolish things; and most introverts can learn to function as extroverts for a limited time. "I love the process of preparing a sermon," said one shy student, "and I'm starting to feel more comfortable actually preaching it. But it exhausts me, and after the service I have to go home and crash." Another said, "I experience the same thing. Preaching really wears me out because you have to be 'up' for so long, plus nerves exhaust you."

There are regional and cultural differences at work, too. When I taught preaching in Georgia, students who had been raised on revivalistic preaching regularly needed to be cautioned to hold back a bit, at least at the beginning of the sermon. In Northern New England, where people can be more reserved, only once has a group I have led had to tell a preaching classmate that his delivery was too animated. Generally, they ask one another to speak out and use more gestures. Fred Craddock, raised in the South, has commented that he was not born with the natural gifts he observed in other successful male preachers: the deep voice, the large personality, and impressive frame. But this caused him to have to work harder, learning how to craft a story that drew from real life, and preach a sermon that did not tip its hand until the very end. He might have felt more at home as a preacher had he been born among the Northern Congregationalists, but would he have become so good?

PAUL ADMITS BEING AFRAID OF PREACHING

Friends, when I came and told you the mystery that God had shared with us, I didn't use big words or try to sound wise. In fact, while I was with you, I made up my mind to speak only about Jesus Christ, who had been nailed to a cross. At first, I was weak and trembling with fear. When I talked with you or preached, I didn't try to prove anything by sounding wise. I simply let God's Spirit show his power. That way you would have faith because of God's power and not because of human wisdom. (1 Corinthians 2:1-5 CEV)

Be More than Yourself in the Pulpit

So, when it comes to sermon delivery, use what God gave you and work hard on the rest. Here just being you may not be enough. You may need to stretch out with your feelings more than seems quite natural. Too many sermons are delivered with all the passion of the local weather forecast. They are "Accurate and Dependable," full of earnest concern about why we should be convinced that the world is falling apart, or that God loves us dearly, but they do not move us out of the seat to want to do anything about it. Our image of public speaking today comes more from the screen in our living rooms than the live theatre, the campaigning politician, and the passionate social reformer. Television reduces complex events to a sound bite and gives us power over even the most gripping personalities. Professional talkers project themselves from inside a box that can be muted or turned off completely. Compelling human dramas and stories can be paused, replayed, or fast-forwarded, giving us the illusion that life is under our control. Our emotional responses to the images are therefore muted. When we see dead bodies from a faraway war, we rarely cry. Sitcom producers know that they have to supply the laugh track because we won't laugh out loud ourselves.

But put us in a room with a passionate speaker and we may light up. The deep memories of sitting around campfires and swapping stories come back to us. Our insides rise and fall with the fortunes of the storyteller. We warm ourselves at the fire of the engaging personality; we become angry with a person with whom we disagree. We rediscover a part of life that we cannot control so we are more likely to react emotionally to it. Perhaps preachers are right to be anxious because preaching involves a level of emotional honesty and intimacy that is increasingly rare in our culture. Most congregations, however, are desperately hungry to be moved.

Some Pointed Advice for Good Sermon Embodiment

In the Study
- Preach sermons that are meaningful to you, personally. If you feel like what you have to say is important, that will come across.

- Write your sermon in a conversational tone, using uncomplicated short sentences and phrases. Write for the ear.

On Sunday Morning
- Eat sparingly the morning before you preach. Avoid "phlegmy" foods like milk.
- Allow yourself plenty of time for prayer or a time of solitude before the service.
- Attend to the hymns and prayers of the worship service. This will help you remember that the presence of God in the room does not depend on your sermon.
- Take your time as you move to the pulpit. Take a good breath and feel your connectedness with the earth, the room, and the people.
- Adjust the microphone if you have one.
- Look up and make eye contact. Be patient for the room to settle down before you begin.
- Speak clearly and enunciate carefully. Remember that folks who have a hard time hearing are more likely to complain of indistinct words than of inadequate volume.
- Use the full range of expression available to you. Start low in pitch, and go slowly, allowing room for your voice and pacing to rise as you hit the high points of your sermon.
- Do not be afraid of showing strong feelings as you preach. The most natural and engaging delivery will come when you are re-experiencing the sermon as you preach it.
- Vary the rhythm. Let there be times in your sermon when you slow down, speed up, or—pause. A sermon whose pace continues uninterrupted will cause minds to wander as surely as those of drivers who never let the odometer waver from sixty-five.

Gestures

The most convincing gestures are those that arise naturally from your involvement in the sermon. Consider how the finest musicians let their whole bodies play the music they are making. Don't choreograph movements, but don't keep your hands glued to the pulpit or your side either. Paying attention to the gestures we use in the pulpit is a good way to find out about what the fundamental intent or purpose of our sermon is, or to what part of the listener the message is addressed.

Jana Childers, in *Performing the Word: Preaching as Theatre*, notes very helpfully that different kinds of preachers tend to have different body language styles: Head-oriented people use finger gestures, like pointing, and eye movements to emphasize their line of thinking. Heart-centered people us more open hand gestures, lively facial expressions, and meaningful pauses. A heart-centered preacher might extend the arm and open the palm when she or he wants to make an appeal to a congregation, like she is a host inviting the congregation to a more intimate circle of friends. Gut-centered people are more likely to use large full-bodied gestures and big arm movements that reflect the big emotions they are feeling inside and the changes of behavior they are trying to promote. As we noted earlier, each of these styles can be effective, but they are different and they seek to move people in different ways. If you don't know what your default mode tends to be, ask someone to observe your gestures for these typical patterns.

Prayer Before the Sermon

For some preachers a prayer before the sermon is absolutely essential to set the tone. Many pray extemporaneously while preachers in liturgical traditions may cross themselves and offer their sermons in the name of the Trinity before they begin. Many preachers today use a formula based on Psalm 19:14: "Let the words of my mouth and the meditation of my heart be acceptable to you, O LORD, my rock and my redeemer." It has become, well, formulaic; and most people change it to something like "the meditations of all our hearts" anyway. I do not pray aloud right before I preach. I believe that it undercuts the fact that the entire worship service is a setting of prayer and puts my own piety on display. Different preachers have different feelings about this, however. My opinion is that it is better to let the sermon be presented as a part of the worship service rather then set it off as something unique by a special prayer.

After the Sermon

Trust God and let it go. If you are conducting the rest of the service, too, don't try to compensate for, continue, or correct your sermon in the words of the pastoral prayer or the benediction. Let each element of the service function in the way it was supposed to function, not be a mini-sermon in itself or a reiteration of what you said.

With so many worship resources available, the fashion these days is to design a worship "experience" around a particular theme, making every prayer, hymn, and utterance fit the theme. Like all fashions, it has its strengths and weaknesses. The desire to bring unity to the worship experience, however, is too often interpreted by pastors to mean trying to make the service fit the sermon. The impression it may leave on the worshiper is that from the moment the hour begins until its end we are being preached at. Rather than allowing us to encounter God, we encounter the earnest intentions of the preacher. So trust the deep rhythm of the church year, trust the people, trust that God can speak to us in the varied words and actions and silences of the rest of the worship service. Trust the sermon once it is over, and let it go.

The Flop

The saying goes that there are three kinds of sailors: those who have run their boats aground, those who will run aground, and liars. The same can be said about preachers. As a beginning sailor who cruises the rocky Maine coast, I am grateful that books on sailing give specific advice about what to do when you run aground. Strangely, however, few preaching books make any comment on sermons that run aground. But it happens to all of us eventually; we preach a flop or at least bore folks to sleep. Some preachers are so caught up in themselves they don't even recognize they've run aground. Unless you are obtuse, however, you will notice that you are floundering in a sermon, even if you aren't sure why. So what to do when you are delivering a sermon that is hitting the rocks? Here are some options:

- Stay the course: keep forging ahead with the sermon if you feel confident that there is better sailing to come. So maybe the long excursus about King Ashurbanipal wasn't as good an idea in real life as it seemed in the study, but the rest of what you have to say about the contemporary relevance of Nahum should strike fire in your congregation's heart.
- Check your depth and try to re-float: shift the balance of your sermon by pausing and restating as simply as possible the main idea of your sermon: "now stay with me for a moment, what I'm trying to do is . . . ." In some congregations, particularly smaller ones, you can even ask for some feedback: "This is a hard passage to understand, are you with me or do I need to come at it from a different angle?" Most congregations I've met would be thrilled to participate in the creation of the sermon in this way. But be careful to use this technique for the sake of the sermon, not to deal with your insecurities. That is, ask whether the sermon is clear, not whether they think you are doing OK.
- Jettison weight: Sermons, like boats, usually get stuck because they are too heavy. Be willing to jettison some of the weight, lighten up, and move quickly to another part of the sermon.
- Tie it down and wait for the next tide: Just bring the sermon to an end with as much grace as you can muster, and wait for the next time to roll around.

Generally, the more you regard a sermon as a conversation that you are having with your congregation rather than a performance you have to get through no matter what, the more you will be able to respond to times when the conversation dies. After all, what do you do at a party when the conversation goes flat? Folks who are anxious about themselves talk too much or too little; those who are interested in other people show it by asking questions and telling good stories.

So here is a final word for self-forgetfulness—we can't be too preoccupied with how we are coming across while we are actually preaching. Be yourself and try to enjoy the moment. Be prepared, love God, and love those to whom you are preaching, and you can hardly go wrong.

CHAPTER 11

Feedback Loops

Sermon Reactions

Now your sermon is over. Assuming they have not risen up to cast you over the brow of a hill, the congregation is saying a creed or singing a hymn. Your body relaxes and the buzz of excitement begins to wear off. If you think it has gone well you are probably able to focus your energy anew on the rest of the worship service and join your congregation in exuberant and heartfelt praise. If you think the sermon has flopped you may be distracted from the rest of worship by your anxieties and questions. That is to say, you are human, and you are understandably concerned with whether your sermon has been well received by others, was considered by the congregation to be faithful, moving, and true. It is time to get honest and helpful feedback on your sermon, not to reassure your anxieties or stroke your ego, but to help you become a better preacher. The first two feedback loops happen spontaneously and are almost always present. The last two require some work on your part but are well worth the effort.

Sermons in the Bible elicit a great many responses. Note that a successful sermon cannot always be measured by how nicely people talk about you after it is over!

- "And the people of Nineveh believed God; they proclaimed a fast, and everyone, great and small, put on sackcloth" (Jonah 3:5).
- "When they heard this, all in the synagogue were filled with rage. They got up, drove him out of town, and led him to the brow of the hill on which their town was built, so that they might hurl him off the cliff" (Luke 4:28-29).
- "While Peter was still speaking, the Holy Spirit fell upon all who heard the word" (Acts 10:44).
- "When they heard of the resurrection of the dead, some scoffed; but others said, 'We will hear you again about this'" (Acts 17:32).
- "A young man named Eutychus, who was sitting in the window, began to sink off into a deep sleep while Paul talked still longer" (Acts 20:9).

Feedback Loop 1: Self-awareness

The first layer of feedback for any sermon is the loop of self-criticism that goes on in your head during and after the sermon. Did I say what I wanted to say? Did the congregation look bored or interested? Did they respond the way I had hoped or expected? Did I make any serious mistakes along the way? It's said the best version of your sermon is the one you preach to yourself on the drive home. You will make judgments about your preaching and it is an inevitable and important part of learning how to preach better. But it is crucial to remember that of all the feedback loops, this is the least important one. Your sermon is what is heard by your congregation, not what you actually said or what you intended to say. Sometimes, the sermon over which you sweat bullets will be the one that moves the congregation most deeply. And the one that you feel most confident about will crash and burn. It's called the working of the Holy Spirit, which blows where it will, and it is proof that the best the preacher can strive to do is work hard and be faithful and leave the rest up to God.

Feedback Loop 2:
On the Way Out the Door

People who hear your sermons will almost always be extremely kind. The first few times you preach, your hearers will bend over backwards to say positive and encouraging things to you—indeed they will be very impressed that you have taken such a large leap from pew to pulpit. This is a measure of God's grace to us as new preachers.

But as you continue to preach, and as people become more used to seeing you in that role, you will probably notice that the tenor of their comments changes. More often than not, they will simply shake your hand and give you an inscrutable look, and tell you, "nice sermon," or "I liked your sermon." Occasionally a person will stop, hold your hand more earnestly, and say, "That is exactly what I needed to hear this morning," or "I loved that story you told about the kid on the tricycle, it reminded me of my uncle Bob," but even these welcome comments won't help you much as you begin to prepare for your next sermon.

Another thing to keep in mind is that if you are like most preachers I know, you will spend far more emotional energy on one critical remark you hear than on the ninety-nine positive comments that people give you. When I was a student pastor in exurban Atlanta, one man in the congregation used to get up, go outside, and smoke a cigarette while I was preaching. He would come back in again and sit down just about the time I was finished. He never said a word, but every time that happened I felt terrible. Fifteen years later that sticks out more in my mind than the many compliments I received at the door of that church. So, while comments on the way out the door are a valuable first glance at how your sermon may have been heard, they can only really be of limited help as you learn to become a better preacher. To get more substantial responses, it is important for you to engineer more formal feedback methods.

"My first preaching confrontation was with a woman who told me quite emphatically that I should be preaching about hell and punishment for sinning. . . . I let her go on; and when she was finished, I simply said there was only one judge and that was God and I didn't purport to know the mind of God. So all I could preach was the Gospel of Jesus Christ, and that is God's grace and loving our neighbors. She didn't say a word, . . . but she comes to church every Sunday and loves me in spite of my theology!"

(A Local United Methodist Lay Pastor)

Feedback Loop 3: Save and Review

If you have typed up notes or a manuscript for your sermon, you need to find a system to file them for future reference. Computers are wonderful for this, as long as the file you keep has any last-minute chicken scratchings you made on the paper you actually took into the pulpit with you—and, as long as you remember to back up your files safely. Most preachers also use a simple three-ring binder to keep those notes and sermons in place and arrange their sermons by date, by scripture text, or by the lectionary calendar. Use whatever system seems best to you.

I have found it a useful practice to write down my own comments and any particularly meaningful comments that I have gathered from the first two feedback loops on the sermon and file them with the sermon itself. Then, when I go back some day to read the sermon, I will have some record of the immediate reactions the sermon engendered. Occasionally, you will want to go back and read your growing sermon collection and learn from it by asking these kinds of questions:

1. Do I fall into any predictable patterns or traps in my preaching? For example, do I always preach from the Gospels, or start every sermon with a funny story?

2. Do my reasoning and theology seem as sound to me now as they did when I first preached the sermon?
3. Have I grown in my ability to interpret scripture and speak my heart clearly and with passion?
4. Are there ways that I could improve the sermon if I were to preach it again?

Looking back at your own sermons can be both sobering and encouraging. At times you will be surprised that you said such thoughtful and beautiful things; at other times you will be appalled.

Begin the practice of audio or video taping your sermons. Many congregations make audiotapes already as a ministry to members who are unable to come to church on Sundays. If so, just ask for an extra tape to be made so that you can hear yourself. If not, a simple audiocassette tape recorder is inexpensive and simple to operate. A video camera can be set up on a tripod and run unobtrusively by a willing member of the congregation. It is often a shock to see or hear yourself on tape for the first time, but this is perhaps the best way to get a realistic assessment of what it is like to be in the pew listening to you preach.

Feedback Loop 4:
Mentors, Groups, and Surveys

Try to arrange a time for careful feedback from people that you trust: senior pastors, good friends, or a small group that will work with you. If you are fortunate enough to have a ministry mentor, ask him or her to focus some time with you specifically on preaching. Some new preachers develop feedback groups with other new preachers and bring tapes or deliver sermons to one another. Others gather a willing group from the congregation to participate in the sermon evaluation and planning process.

The United Methodist Bishop Joseph Sprague became one of that denomination's most inspiring preachers partly because he met weekly with parishioners to participate in the preaching ministry of the church. Meeting early in the morning before the work hour began, they would first give him feedback on the previous week's sermon by offering "Wish you had" and "Wish you hadn't" comments. Then they would discuss their questions and interpretations of the upcoming lectionary text, which would allow Sprague to develop sermons that connected with the real lives of the congregation.

Here is the most important thing for you to do during these feedback sessions: be quiet and listen. You will be tempted to explain to others what you were trying to do. That is irrelevant. All that matters is what was actually heard. In my classes, we have gradually developed the following system that works really well because it encourages open dialogue and ensures that the preacher gets the best possible feedback.

1. Gather the listeners into a circle with the preacher and name someone as a group leader (not the preacher) to direct the conversation.
2. Name another person (not the preacher) to take notes of the conversation.
3. The preacher must remain quiet and listen during the feedback session.
4. Take about ten minutes to answer this question: What made this sermon effective? The leader should make sure that the group talks about the main idea, the purpose of the sermon, the use of scripture, language, illustrations, and so on.
5. Then spend about ten minutes answering the question: What would have made this sermon more effective?
6. Members of the group should direct their comments to the sermon, not to the preacher. Instead of: "I loved the story you told about Spot and Jane," say: "The opening story

about Spot and Jane was effective because . . . " Instead of: "I was annoyed when you rocked back and forth in your sermon," say: "The preacher's movements were distracting because. . . ."

7. When the leader thinks the conversation has run its course, if there is time, the leader may ask the preacher if she or he would like to summarize what they heard or ask clarifying, nondefensive questions. For example: "Joan, you mentioned that you were distracted by my hand motions. Can you show me what you meant?" or, "Fred, I wasn't sure what you meant when you said you didn't agree with the way I interpreted that verse."

It will probably take several sessions before a mentor or group will develop the trust to speak candidly with you, but they will only do this if you demonstrate an unwavering commitment to listening openly. Yet following this exercise or one like it will make a huge difference in the ability of the congregation to listen to sermons well, and will be a true gift to you as a preacher.

Another way to get feedback on a sermon is to distribute brief surveys to the congregation before the sermon starts. If you explain that you are a new preacher who is trying to learn to preach better, you will find that most people are very happy to help in this way. Here is a simple questionnaire that you can use.

SERMON QUESTIONNAIRE

As a new preacher, it helps me to get as much feedback as possible. Thank you for taking some moments after the sermon to answer a few brief questions. Please put this in the basket near the door as you leave.

Date:_____

Sermon Title: _____

Biblical Text: _____

What did you hear as the main idea of the sermon?

What other ideas did you hear?

Was there a particular illustration or story that you remember? Why?

Did the sermon use the Bible effectively? Why or why not?

What did you hear this sermon calling you to do?

How was my delivery? My use of the voice, gestures, the microphone? Was there anything that I did that was particularly effective? Distracted from the message?

What else could make this sermon more effective?

Participating in the preaching evaluation and learning process will do wonders for the sense of ownership of the whole congregation of its ministry of the Word. Not only will it help you preach better, it will open the eyes of others to the prayerful thought and hard work that preaching requires for it to fulfill its task faithfully. Perhaps it will spur the interest of others to think about whether they may be called to this vital ministry of bringing good news through preaching.

CHAPTER 12

Words at the Door

Speaking for God?

It was the final meeting of our semester's preaching class. It seemed hard to believe that we were finishing our course even though we still had so much to learn together about preaching. A student asked, "How does one become certain of divine direction? How does one find the assurance to speak for God? I don't want to keep silent when God would have me speak, but even more do I fear to speak when God would have me keep silent." Other students nodded and echoed his anxiety about the gravity of preaching. It was interesting that these questions came up powerfully on the very last day of our semester's preaching class. This was a group that had deeply matured in its preaching over thirteen weeks. The students were choosing important things to say in their sermons and were saying them well. They could feel the power that was being generated in strong preaching and the effect they were having on one another. They were taking risks, being themselves, and giving their testimonies. It was exhilarating but frightening. Now that they knew a little bit about how to craft a sermon, would they succumb to the temptation to use words about God to push a personal opinion? Would they preach themselves or the Hope that is within them?

The best preachers are those who worry about these profound questions. I knew simply by listening to these thoughtful students that they would be good ministers and preachers. They were making the journey from pew to pulpit with integrity and love. I could look forward to hearing them mature as preachers in the years to come, because they understand what a risky business it is to love God's people by words carefully chosen and proclaimed with passion.

A Blessing

It is my hope that at least at some point during your sermon you will have noticed our attentive faces and understood how much your preaching means to us. We are amazed at what has happened in the very midst of our community. You used to sit quietly where we are sitting now and yet on this day you are preaching with us. I hope you noticed in our faces that we were not sitting there evaluating your voice, judging your insight into the biblical text, or trying to decipher your sermon form. Mostly, we were just profoundly grateful for the hard work you have clearly done on our behalf. You have wrestled with the Bible, thought about God's life in the world, and unguardedly shared your testimony. Thank you for your willingness to be transparent to the work of the Spirit. Thank you for raising our deepest thoughts into sacred speech, for increasing our desire to love God and neighbor, and for moving us to live by faith. May God bless you for responding to the call.

Select Bibliography for New Preachers

Allen, Ronald J. *Preaching the Topical Sermon*. Louisville: Westminster/John Knox Press, 1992.

———. *Preaching: An Essential Guide*. Nashville: Abingdon Press, 2003.

———, ed. *Patterns of Preaching*. St. Louis: Chalice Press, 1998.

Brown, Teresa L. Fry. *Weary Throats and New Songs: Black Women Proclaiming God's Word*. Nashville: Abingdon Press, 2003.

Buttrick, David. *A Captive Voice: The Liberation of Preaching*. Louisville: Westminster/John Knox Press, 1994.

Childers, Jana. *Performing the Word: Preaching as Theatre*. Nashville: Abingdon Press, 1998.

———, ed. *Birthing the Sermon: Women Preachers on the Creative Process*. St. Louis: Chalice Press, 2001.

Craddock, Fred. *Preaching*. Nashville: Abingdon Press, 1985.

Crawford, Evans E. *The Hum: Call and Response in African American Preaching*. Nashville: Abingdon Press, 1995.

Dowis, Richard. *The Lost Art of the Great Speech: How to Write One, How to Deliver It*. New York: ANACOM, 2000.

Harris, James Henry. *The Word Made Plain: The Power and Promise of Preaching*. Minneapolis: Fortress Press, 2004.

Jacks, G. Robert. *Just Say the Word: Writing for the Ear*. Grand Rapids: Eerdmans, 1996.

LaRue, Cleophus J., ed. *Power in the Pulpit: How America's Most

Effective Black Preachers Prepare their Sermons. Louisville: Westminster/John Knox Press, 2002.

Long, Thomas G. *The Witness of Preaching.* Louisville: Westminster/John Knox Press, 1989.

Lowery, Eugene. *The Homiletical Plot: The Sermon as Narrative Art Form.* Expanded Edition. Louisville: Westminster/John Knox Press, 2001 (1980).

Massey, James Earl. *Designing the Sermon: Order and Movement in Preaching.* Ed. William D. Thompson. Nashville: Abingdon Press, 1980.

McClure, John S., ed. *Best Advice for Preaching.* Minneapolis: Fortress Press, 1998.

McKinney, Lora-Ellen. *View from the Pew: What Preachers Can Learn from Church Members.* Valley Forge, Pa.: Judson Press, 2004.

Mitchell, Henry H. *Black Preaching: The Recovery of a Powerful Art.* Nashville: Abingdon Press, 1990.

Nieman, James R., and Thomas G. Rogers. *Preaching to Every Pew: Cross-Cultural Strategies.* Minneapolis: Fortress Press, 2001.

Norén, Carol M. *The Woman in the Pulpit.* Nashville: Abingdon Press, 1992.

Parachini, Patricia A. *Guide for Lay Preachers.* Chicago: Liturgy Training Publications, 2000.

Schlafer, David J. *Your Way with God's Word: Discovering Your Distinctive Preaching Voice.* Cambridge: Cowley, 1995.

Taylor, Barbara Brown. *The Preaching Life.* Cambridge: Cowley, 1993.

Tisdale, Leonora Tubbs. *Preaching as Local Theology and Folk Art.* Minneapolis: Fortress Press, 1997.

Troeger, Thomas H. *Ten Strategies for Preaching in a MultiMedia Culture.* Nashville: Abingdon Press, 1996.

Wagley, Laurence A. *Preaching with the Small Congregation.* Nashville: Abingdon Press, 1989.

Ward, Richard. *Speaking of the Holy: The Art of Communication in Preaching.* St. Louis: Chalice Press, 2001.

Webb, Joseph M. *Preaching Without Notes.* Nashville: Abingdon, 2001.

Willimon, William H. *Pastor: The Theology and Practice of Ordained Ministry.* Nashville: Abingdon Press, 2002.

Wilson, Paul Scott. *The Four Pages of the Sermon: A Guide to Biblical Preaching.* Nashville: Abingdon Press, 1999.